THE 100+ SERIES™

Reproducible Activities

The Writer's Express

Grade 4-5

By
Lorilynn

Cover Illustration by
Jeff Van Kanegan

Inside Illustrations by
Kathryn Marlin

Published by Instructional Fair • TS Denison
an imprint of

 **McGraw-Hill**
Children's Publishing

ABOUT THE AUTHOR

Lorilynn has been a teacher of elementary- and middles school-aged children for 20 years. She had worked in both public and private schools across the United States. She earned her Bachelor of Arts in psychology and her Master of Arts in educational psychology from the University of Michigan. She is currently a freelance writer and educational therapist in Ojai, California. In addition to educational books, she writes poetry, short stories, and articles for journals.

CREDITS

Author: Lorilynn
Cover Design: Jeff Van Kanegan
Inside Illustrations: Kathryn Marlin

McGraw-Hill
Children's Publishing

A Division of The McGraw-Hill Companies

Published by Instructional Fair • TS Denison
An imprint of McGraw-Hill Children's Publishing
Copyright © 1999 McGraw-Hill Children's Publishing

Send all inquiries to:
McGraw-Hill Children's Publishing
3195 Wilson Drive NW
Grand Rapids, Michigan 49544

The Writer's Express—grades 4-5
ISBN: 1-56822-862-7

3 4 5 6 7 8 9 PHXBK 07 06 05 04 03 02

TABLE OF CONTENTS

Section Four: True Stories

Section Five: Story Elements

Section Six: Genres

Section Seven: Mechanics

Appendix

Answer Key

INTRODUCTION

Writing is about conveying experiences, transmitting images, and generating feelings. Helping students become writers means immersing them in sensory experiences and training them to translate these encounters into words that will recreate the experiences for the reader. No easy task, to be sure!

Often, it helps students to realize that writing is very much like directing a movie. Just like a director, a writer has to find ways to evoke in his or her audience the same vision the writer has in mind. The tools available for doing this with movies, however, are much more varied than the tools that can be used in books. While the movie director has audio, video, and special effects, the only tool a writer has is words. It is therefore critical to a writer's work that word choices be effective. Similarly, writing is improved if the many different ways of using language are explored, understood, and utilized in composition.

The Writer's Express offers a unique series of activities designed to meet these goals. While any section or page may be used independently of the others, you will find that using them in the order in which they are presented will provide a comprehensive picture of the writing process for your students. Beginning with experiencing the five senses, the first section, "Creative Writer's Toolbox," moves on to examine specific tools of language. From there, the role of grammatical concepts in expanding writing is explored. The final portion of this section stresses the importance of using aids such as the dictionary and the thesaurus in the task of writing.

The second section, "Poetry," provides opportunities for students to use what was learned in the first section as the concepts relate to poems. This is a particularly good progression because the tools of language are especially critical to poem construction.

Section Three, "Shorts," highlights the smaller pieces that will eventually be combined to produce a larger work. These activities have proven especially instructive to students when they have a chance to share their work, accept constructive criticism, and rewrite using this feedback. Spending some time on this section will allow students to pay attention to the details they will need later when they write stories or essays.

"True Stories," found in Section Four, concerns fairly short pieces of writing which require developed thought and a product which is informative and thoroughly written. The activities in this section all pertain to factual forms of writing, rather than fiction, which is addressed in Section Six.

The elements contained in all stories are examined in detail in Section Five, "Story Elements." Here you will find information and activities designed to help students focus on each aspect involved in writing an interesting story. From deciding what to write to bringing the story to an appropriate end, students will practice each critical part of story creation.

Section Six, "Genres," offers practice in a variety of types of writing. In this portion, you will find starter ideas, samples, and independent activities for follow-up work. As is true in many places in *The Writer's Express,* working with classmates to develop and critique writing is an integral component of this section.

In Section Seven, "Mechanics," activities which deal with drafts, critiques, editing, and proof-reading are presented. The last section, which contains the Appendix, provides both students and teachers with additional samples, guidelines, and planners.

While this book has attempted to provide an array of materials for writing, you may wish to select several sections and expand them more in depth on your own. *The Writer's Express* is a resource for you and your students to enjoy. Use it as a springboard to stimulate and promote creativity as your students learn to be the best writers they can be!

Section 1

Creative Writer's Toolbox

SEE IT

What we see is perhaps the easiest aspect of our senses to communicate in writing. One of the most difficult parts of writing, however, is communicating to the reader exactly *how*, or in what way, we saw what we saw. A writer not only wants a reader to "see" the picture that is being painted, but to *respond* to it as well—to *feel* something about what is being seen. To do this, a writer must watch his or her subject very carefully. Words that describe its physical appearance, its actions, and its intentions will help the reader understand the subject in the way we want it understood.

For example, if you are writing a story about young horses playing in a field together, you will need to watch the horses at play. You can go to a farm and look at them or you can watch a film about them. If you do not watch them, however, you will not notice the little things that you need to notice about young horses to write well about them. Even if you have seen horses play before, you need to watch again to refresh your memory and take some notes.

When taking notes on a subject, jot down words or phrases that seem to describe best what you see. Notes on young horses might include the following phrases:

Describing the actions:
   frisky   *playful chasing*   *graceful prancing*   *rearing happily*

Describing the horses:
   • *black with four white socks, white star, large wild brown eyes, stand-up mane, wisp of a tail, colt, long spindly legs*
   • *white with black leopard spots on rump; striped hooves; black-and-white hairs mixed in mane and tail; kind, happy eyes; filly; smaller than black colt*

From these notes, the author can write about the horses later and still transmit to the reader the scene that was witnessed. This is much like the way an artist begins a picture. First, the artist sketches the essential parts of the subject. Later on, the details are added to complete the picture.

On Your Own

Spend 15 to 20 minutes watching a subject. Take notes on the actions of the subject and the physical description of the subject. Be as complete as possible with your notes, including even the smallest details which might help your reader visualize the scene. Later, use your notes as the beginning of a story.

HEAR IT

Focusing on sounds in writing greatly adds to the reader's sense of what is going on. However, translating what we hear into words can be quite a task. To illustrate this, choose one of the following and explain the sound in writing as if it were part of a story.

an airplane   a songbird   a lonely calf   a fire engine

_____

_____

_____

_____

_____

_____

How did you do? Did you find it difficult? Did it take quite a few words to get the sound "heard"? Here is a "sound" example using an ambulance siren:

Off in the distance, a faint whine could be heard. Gradually it crescendoed into a wail and finally became a howling shriek. As it neared the intersection, the loud horn blared and I jumped back farther away from the curb. The ambulance continued its frantic pace down the street, and the ear-piercing siren quickly faded away.

✍ On Your Own

Choose a place to sit and listen to the sounds around you. Close your eyes for at least five minutes and discover what you can tell about your environment from what you hear. What kind of sounds are you listening to? (City sounds? Forest sounds? Human sounds?) Do the sounds belong to living or nonliving things? (A rabbit? Traffic? The wind?) Where are the sounds? (Near you? In the distance? Up in the sky?) What do the sounds tell you? (Something is hunting for food? Someone is approaching? A storm is coming?)

When you are finished listening, describe the sounds you heard in writing. Try to make the reader hear exactly what you heard and feel exactly as you felt while you were sitting there listening.

Touch It

There is nothing like touching something when you really want to understand it. The sensation of touch communicates many signals and feelings to the human brain. Things that are hot, slimy, soft, or bumpy not only tell us how they feel to our hands, but elicit emotions as well. Here are some responses we might have to the words just mentioned: hot—pain, slimy—yuck, soft—good, bumpy—strange.

Work with a partner to describe objects only by touching them. Close your eyes and ask your partner to choose an item to place in your hands. "See" the item by touching it carefully. Say the words that come to mind as your hands examine the object. Your partner will write down these words. Then, without opening your eyes, guess what the object is. Here is an example:

small, metal, hard, ridges on the edges, round, raised design, cold to touch
a quarter

Do this several times with different objects. Then give your partner some objects to describe while you do the recording.

✍ On Your Own

Using the words you used to describe one of your objects, imagine that this object is the focus of an opening to a story. Write a paragraph that details what the object feels like. Do not reveal what the object is until the end of your paragraph—or leave it up to the reader to guess its true identity. Then exchange your story starter with your partner and each of you can write a second paragraph. Here is an example using the quarter above:

Jerry slipped his hand into his pocket and felt the cold, metal object once more. He took it out and studied the raised design on the front and back. Slowly he ran his fingernail over the ridges on the edges, feeling a shiver shudder through his body as he did so. He rolled it from the palm of one hand to the other. Then he glanced at the blind man waiting patiently on the curb in front of him. It was Jerry's last quarter and he had had no supper that day. He held the coin between his thumb and forefinger, hesitating. Suddenly, as if inspired, he strode forward and dropped the money into the blind man's cup. "God bless you, son," the blind man said, never lifting his head.

TASTE IT

Our sense of taste is very powerful. When we try a new food, it does not take us long to decide whether we like it or not. Almost immediately, our brain responds with the judgment "good" or "bad," and so we learn quickly which foods we like to bring home from the grocery store. Because the sense of taste is so individual, it is important to the development of a character in writing. Does this character like spinach or hate it? What is her favorite flavor of ice cream or candy? Does she eat when she is angry or nervous? The answers to these questions will help a reader understand the character more completely. Before you can build your character's taste buds, however, you need to be aware of your own. Try the activity below to help you learn to describe what you are tasting.

It is a bit of a challenge to isolate the taste sensation. Close your eyes and hold your nose so that you are only tasting the food. The sense of smell plays an important role in identifying foods, so it is necessary to block it off for this tasting activity. Ask your partner to place a piece of food in your mouth. Eat it slowly, thinking about how it tastes and feels in your mouth. When you are finished, describe the food to your partner, who will write down your responses. Make a guess about what the food was. Here is an example:

small, round, rubbery, sweet and sour, more sweet than sour, squishy when bitten,
firm on outside, mushy on inside, two seeds on inside
a purple grape

Do this several times with different foods. Then give your partner some foods to try while you do the recording.

 On Your Own

Using the words you used to describe one of your foods, imagine that a character in your story is eating something. Write a paragraph that details what the character is tasting and how he or she reacts to that taste. Here is an example using the grape above:

Miranda stopped picking the fruit and popped one of the large purple grapes into her mouth. She rolled it around on her tongue for a moment, enjoying the rubbery feel of its cool surface. Then she bit into it, squishing out the sweet-sour insides and chewing it up slowly. "Yummy," she said as she pulled another grape from its stem, "I just love grapes!"

SMELL IT

When the aroma of something we love comes drifting down the street to us, we immediately take notice. Baked goods often draw us in as we pass by bakeries. As the smell of their favorite brew floats through the air, coffee lovers find themselves wandering into coffee shops. And who can resist the lure of popcorn popping when entering a movie theater? Our noses also tell us when something is unpleasant. Passing a garbage dump, a barnyard, or a sewer are all experiences that will send us rushing to close the windows of a car or hold our noses in protest.

Like all of our senses, the sense of smell does more than notify us of something we like or dislike. It also triggers emotions. The scent of someone's perfume can remind us of a person we love and instantly transport our minds to the last time we were with that person. Likewise, a smell we find disgusting can remind us of unhappy times, such as the last time we had to eat a food we did not like.

When you write, describing smells and the emotions they bring out in a character will allow your reader to have a better sense of a character or a scene you have created in your story. To gain some practice in writing about smells, try the activity below.

Close your eyes and ask your partner to hold an object under your nose. Sniff it several times, thinking about what emotions and reactions this smell brings to you. Describe the smell and your feelings about the smell to your partner, who will write down your responses. Make a guess about what the object was. Here is an example:

> *strong, sweet, a lovely smell, reminds me of perfume,*
> *makes me feel both happy and sad*
> *roses*

Do this several times with different objects. Then give your partner some objects to smell while you do the recording.

On Your Own

Using the words you used to describe one of the objects, imagine that a character in your story is smelling something. Write a paragraph that details what the character is smelling and how he or she reacts to that smell. Here is an example using the roses above:

Allie stopped walking as she passed by the rose bed. The wonderful sweet smell of the flowers beckoned to her. She stooped down and drew a lovely pink rose to her face. Its perfumed scent enveloped her, and tears came to her eyes as she remembered her mother's love for these beautiful flowers. For a moment, she was lost in time, recalling her mother's gentle voice and seeing again her long, elegant fingers arrange the bouquet of pink and yellow roses Allie had given her last Mother's Day.

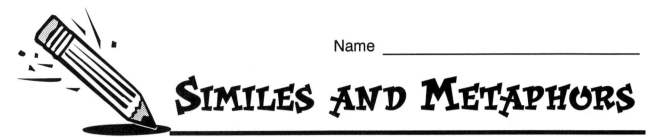

As a writer, you want to help your readers relate to what is happening in your story. An excellent way to do this is through the use of similes and metaphors. *Similes* and *metaphors* show similarities between two things or ideas that are not really very much alike. They do this in different ways.

A *simile* compares things through the use of *like* or *as*. For example:

> Her mother was **as** lovely as a rose.
> Her mother was **like** a rose, beautiful and elegant.

A *metaphor* compares things directly, often using a state of being verb, such as *am, is, are, was,* or *were*. For example:

> Her mother **was** a rose.

In the examples above, the two things that are being compared are the mother and the rose. With the use of either the simile or the metaphor, the reader understands that the mother is similar to a rose—that she is pretty and stylish. That is the purpose of this type of figurative language: to give the reader an image that helps in making the picture clearer. Similes can be made into metaphors and metaphors can be made into similes. The one you choose to use is up to you.

Decide whether the sentences below use similes or metaphors. Write *S* or *M* on the line to the right of each one. Then on the blanks below each sentence, write what the simile or metaphor is comparing.

_____ 1. The wind brushed against his face gently like the breath of a small child.

_____ is being compared to _____.

_____ 2. She was a devil.

_____ is being compared to _____.

_____ 3. As slowly as a turtle, the boy walked up to the chalkboard.

_____ is being compared to _____.

_____ 4. Suddenly, the children were birds, flying free within the fantasy of their minds.

_____ are being compared to _____.

On Your Own

Try writing a paragraph which uses at least two similes and two metaphors to compare things. Be creative and descriptive by choosing your words carefully.

Name _____

PERSONIFICATION

One of the most vivid ways to communicate imagery to your readers is through the use of *personification*.

Personification means giving human qualities to something that is not alive. Here are some examples:

The **siren screamed** loudly, **screeching** at everyone to get out of the way.

Crying crocodile tears, the **clouds** let their **sadness** fall.

The **trees moved their knobby fingers** in the eerie shadows.

In the sentences above, the words that show personification appear in bold letters. Because a siren cannot *really* scream or screech, clouds do not *really* cry or feel sadness, and trees do not *really* have fingers, these are examples of personification.

Underline the examples of personification in the sentences below.

1. The brisk winter air bit at her lungs and she struggled to breathe.
2. The kite reached up to the blue sky, taunting the clouds to follow the path of its playful tail.
3. As morning broke through the fog, the sun smiled brilliantly, warming the beach.
4. The pen leapt out of my hand, as if it had a life of its own.
5. Winding slowly through the woods, the lazy river babbled on senselessly to the nearby trees.

✍ On Your Own

Try writing the beginning of a story using at least two examples of personification. When you are finished, share your work with a friend.

Here are some topics that may help you get started:
the wind on a summer day   the moon on a cold night
a boat on a stormy sea   a car on a mountain road
a hot air balloon in the sky   an avalanche of snow

Assonance and Alliteration

Often thought of as tongue twisters, these two twins of figurative language are very pleasing to the ear. They are frequently used in advertising because the brain is drawn to their sounds. Likewise, using them in your writing will keep your readers more engaged.

Assonance is the repetition of the same vowel sound in words that are close together in a poem or within a sentence. These sounds may be inside the words, as in "make" and "late" or at the beginning of words as in the example below:

Annie always ate apples and apricots.

In this example, *ate* is not included because it has a long "a" sound, while the rest of the words have a short "a" sound.

Alliteration is the repetition of the same consonant sound at the beginning of words in a sentence. For example:

The snake slithered silently on the sand.

In this example, the "s" sound at the beginning of each word makes up the alliteration.

Notice that only the beginning sound needs to be the same in each word. The words do not need to begin with the same letters. Thus, the sentence "The **k**id **k**icked the **c**an into the **c**reek" is an example of alliteration, even though the letters involved are "k" and "c."

Assonance and alliteration are fun to use and help enhance imagery and heighten the interest of readers. Circle the letters used to make assonance and alliteration in the sentences below.

1. Climbing calmly into the car, Katie carried her cat.

2. Whistling wildly through the wind, the rocket whirled upward.

3. Silly Sarah slowly slid sadly through the slime.

4. Edward exited the roller coaster excitedly, exclaiming, "Excellent, excellent!"

✍ On Your Own

Write ten sentences using assonance or alliteration. Choose one of them to develop into a paragraph. Remember that to be effective, these tools must not be overused.

Question: Can you find the alliteration used in the first sentence on this page?

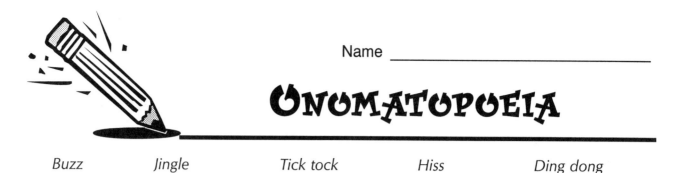

ONOMATOPOEIA

Buzz   Jingle   Tick tock   Hiss   Ding dong

What do these words have in common? What is your response to them as you read? Which of your senses is stimulated by the use of these words?

You probably noticed that all of these words have to do with sound. When creating sound imagery, they are particularly good choices because when you say them out loud, they imitate the sound they are describing. Words that do this are called *onomatopoeias*.

Onomatopoeias add a great deal to writing. They help the reader hear the sounds the writer is trying to convey. Can you think of any other words that are onomatopoeias? Write them on the line below.

_____

Examine these two examples of writing. They describe the same scene. Which example uses an onomatopoeia? How does the onomatopoeia add to the writing?

Example One: *Anna sat by the window, searching the snowy landscape for her father. It was past the time he usually arrived home. What was keeping him? The snow was falling ever more heavily now and she was anxious for him to appear. As she peered through the frosty pane, she saw a faint movement in the distance. Perhaps that was his sleigh.*

Example Two: *Anna sat by the window, searching the snowy landscape for her father. It was past the time he usually arrived home. What was keeping him? The snow was falling ever more heavily now, and she was anxious for him to appear. As she peered through the frosty pane, she saw a faint movement in the distance. She listened hard. Within a few moments she began to hear the pleasant jingle, jingle of sleigh bells. Judging from the tone of the bells, she felt fairly certain that they belonged to her father's sleigh.*

✍ On Your Own

Write two examples of a scene like the ones above. In one of your examples, use an onomatopoeia. Ask a friend to read your writing and identify the onomatopoeia that you used. Discuss how the use of the onomatopoeia makes the images more vivid for the reader.

HYPERBOLE

Do you ever find yourself exaggerating? Do you have a friend who often exaggerates? Exaggerations can be fun to create and humorous to read. They can also be used to emphasize certain points you want to make or to bring a greater sense of drama to your writing.

A *hyperbole* is the use of exaggeration to create a certain effect. You might think of hyperboles as a writer's "special effects" because they have a way of getting ideas across very quickly, just like special effects do in movies. Consider the example below:

Bill slumped sadly in his chair. The mountain of paperwork before him was as tall as the Empire State Building. He knew he would never finish by six o'clock.

What are the words that make up the hyperbole in this example? _____

_____

What is really meant by the hyperbole? _____

_____

Can you think of some sayings we hear often that are hyperboles? Two examples appear below. Write the meaning of each hyperbole on the line below it. Then think of some more hyperboles and write them in the space given.

I'm so hungry, I could eat a horse!

_____

He's as big as a barn!

_____

More hyperboles:

_____

_____

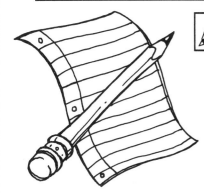

✍ On Your Own

Think about an American legend such as Paul Bunyan or Johnny Appleseed. Legends often contain hyperboles because stories tend to get exaggerated every time they are told again. Work with a partner to write some hyperboles that would help describe a character in one of these legends.

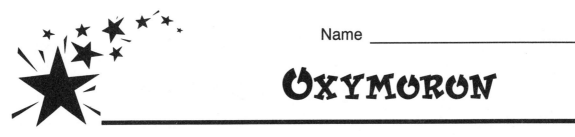

Name _____

OXYMORON

Oxymoron. Have you ever heard of this word? What do you think it means? Write your guess here.

_____

Now look at these examples of oxymorons.

    a bright darkness   *a small giant*   *a thundering silence*

What do all these phrases have in common? After looking at the examples, how would you define an *oxymoron?* _____

_____

An oxymoron is a phrase which contains words that are opposite in meaning, but when put together result in a special idea. Try writing a sentence that uses each oxymoron above.

a bright darkness: _____

_____

a small giant: _____

_____

a thundering silence: _____

_____

Oxymorons are useful in writing both stories and poems. They are another writer's tool that helps create good imagery. Here is a sample from a story. Can you find the oxymoron?

The court jester was dressed in a brilliant purple suit with yellow trim. From his hat hung four tassles, each waving wildly as he performed his antics for the king. Everyone laughed and applauded happily as he back-flipped into the enormous birthday cake. The jester smiled to himself and took a bow, for he knew he was truly a majestic fool.

✍ On Your Own

Make a list of oxymorons. Choose one and write a paragraph or poem which uses it. Share your work with a classmate and discuss the meaning of the oxymoron you used in your work.

RHYME

Words that have the same ending sounds are called *rhyming words*. Most of us have heard rhymes such as "Mother Goose" and "Dr. Seuss" since we were very young. (Did you notice the rhyme in those titles?) Our brains respond well to rhymes. We like the sing-song nature of rhymes, which helps us to remember them. Think of a rhyme that you have heard before. Write it below.

_____

_____

Does your rhyme contain words that rhyme at the end of each line? If so, this is called *end rhyme*. End rhyme is used a great deal in songs and poems and in many young children's books. Commercials also use these types of rhymes to help us remember their products.

Another type of rhyme is *internal rhyme*. When a line of a poem or a sentence in a story contains words that rhyme within that line, it is called *internal rhyme*. Here is an example:

Jill and Jane were on a plane.

The words *Jane* and *plane* rhyme and are in the same line.

A third type of rhyme is *forced rhyme*. Sometimes, in order for our writing to make sense, we have to choose words that almost rhyme. When we do this, we are using forced rhyme. An example of forced rhyme appears below. Can you find it?

Jake lost his coat
When he fell off the boat
This made him cross
For money it cost
To pull him out of the moat.

✍ On Your Own

Write your own rhyming story. Experiment with these three types of rhymes. When you are finished, ask a classmate to identify each type you used. Draw pictures to go with your work.

RHYME SCHEME

The rhyme scheme of a poem describes the pattern of rhyming words. We use lowercase letters to label the rhyme scheme. The last word at the end of the first line receives the letter "a." The last word of the second line, if it rhymes with the first word, also receives the letter "a." If the second word does not rhyme with the first word, however, it receives a "b." The next new rhyme receives a "c," etc.

Limericks are one type of poetry that uses a definite rhyme scheme. The rhyme scheme of a limerick follows the pattern **aabba**. To understand this more completely, look at the limerick below:

To Be Said of Ed	Ending word	Rhyme scheme
There once was a man named Ed	Ed	a
Who had brain cells galore in his head	head	a
And though he was older	older	b
He became ever bolder	bolder	b
About saying what had to be said	said	a

Since *Ed*, *head*, and *said* all rhyme, they receive the same letter: "a." *Older* and *bolder* also rhyme, but they do not rhyme with the other three words, so they receive the letter "b."

Songs often have definite rhyme schemes, too. Here is the chorus to a song. See if you can correctly label its rhyme scheme.

Chorus	Ending word	Rhyme scheme
Snowflakes begin to fall	_____	_____
Winter hears its call	_____	_____
Sleigh bells ring inside my mind	_____	_____
Memories of a happy time	_____	_____

✍ On Your Own

Choose one of your favorite poems or songs and try to label its entire rhyme scheme. If you get all the way to "z" and still have more rhymes, use "aa," "bb," "cc," etc. Exchange papers with a classmate and see if he or she agrees with the way you have labeled your rhyme scheme.

REPETITION

Repetition occurs when sounds, words, phrases, sentences, images, grammatical constructions, or ideas are used more than once in a piece of writing. Repetition is used in many types of writing including poetry, songs, stories, and essays. Repetition can even be visual, such as using a certain number of syllables, words, or lines to create an effect that can be seen. When a writer wants to be certain the reader understands what he or she intended to say, repetition is often the tool that is used.

Below is a poem which uses repetition in several ways. Circle all the examples of repetition that you can find. Then check your work with a classmate and compare results.

did you see the sky
did you see the sky

i chased the sun
all the way home
but
i could not catch
the glorious glow
and
it faded
imperceptibly
yet steadily
away

To consider the effect repetition has on the reader, read the above poem aloud *without* the first two lines. How is the feeling and/or message of the poem different?

✍ On Your Own

Look for some examples of repetition in poetry, songs, or books. Bring in at least two pieces of writing that use repetition and share them with your class. Discuss why the author chose to use repetition at that point in the writing.

STANZA

Stanzas are found in poems. They are somewhat like the paragraphs of a story because each stanza usually contains one basic thought or idea. Stanzas are made up of a certain number of lines and are separated by spaces. Sometimes, entire poems are written in stanzas that are all the same length. Stanzas do not have to use rhyme, but many of them do. Here are two examples:

Example One

Zoe was a puppy so small
She came up to my ankle, that's all!

Example Two

Our teacher, dear old Mr. Fink
Every morning put up such a stink
For, no matter the date
We always came late!

Each of these examples shows one stanza of a poem. Example One is called a *couplet* because it has two lines in its stanza. Example Two is called a *quatrain* because it has four lines in its stanza. Here are the names for stanzas with two to eight lines each:

Two lines: couplet
Three lines: tercet or triplet
Four lines: quatrain
Five lines: cinquain or quintet
Six lines: sestet
Seven lines: heptastitch or septet
Eight lines: octave

On Your Own

Choose one type of stanza from the list above and write a three-stanza poem
or
create a name for a stanza longer than eight lines and write a two-stanza poem using that stanza. All of these names use a prefix that has something to do with the number of lines in the stanza. Follow this pattern when you name your stanza.

SYMBOL

What does the American flag represent? What is the picture of a white dove used to represent? What do you think of when you see a cross? These objects are all symbols.

A *symbol* is anything that stands for or represents something else. In the examples above, the American flag stands for freedom, a white dove for peace, and a cross represents the idea of religion or God.

Writers use symbols, too. A writer does not actually tell the reader what the symbol is, however. Instead, the reader must figure it out. A symbol is different from some of the other language techniques because it usually appears from time to time throughout a story. Often, a concrete symbol may stand for something abstract. Such a symbol was used in the popular movie *Forrest Gump*. In this movie, a floating feather was used to symbolize the idea that people float about in life, without too much control over what happens to them.

Another example of a symbol can be found in John Christopher's book, *The White Mountains*. In this story of life in the future, 13-year-olds are "capped." Being "capped" stands for the loss of a person's ability to think on their own, or a loss of freedom.

On Your Own

Choose a symbol that best describes you. List the reasons this is a good symbol for you. Then create a paragraph using this symbol. An example appears below:

She had dreamt of it again. This time it had been partly hidden by clouds, flying in and out of the mist. It was a silver unicorn, with a golden horn and matching gilded hooves. She tried to keep up with it, but it eluded her and faded away. When she awoke, Marissa had an uneasy feeling that what she sought lay just out of her reach.

What do you think the unicorn might symbolize in this story?_____

_____

What makes you think this? _____

_____

Share your ideas with your class.

Instead of "Said"

In writing *dialogue*, the part of a story that shows someone is talking, a writer often uses the word *said* before or after the spoken part. However, *said* is not the only word that can be used to show speech. Consider the example below.

> *"I am hungry," said Bob.*
> *"I want a hamburger," said Jill.*
> *"Let's go get some food," said Dad.*
> *"Ok," said everyone.*

Said is used too often in this dialogue, and it makes the writing seem boring and dull. Look at the difference in the following example:

> *"I am hungry!" exclaimed Bob.*
> *"I want a hamburger!" wailed Jill.*
> *"Let's go get some food," suggested Dad.*
> *"Ok!" everyone agreed.*

What are some things you find out about the characters or the situation in the second example that you cannot figure out from the first example?

_____

_____

_____

When trying to "paint" a scene for your readers to "see," these more descriptive words can bring a story or poem alive, just like a color television set gives brilliance to the screen. Action words, also known as *verbs*, are particularly critical in a dialogue. They can completely change the "picture" for the reader. When you use words instead of *said*, you provide more clues for your reader. This gives the reader a better understanding of what you are trying to communicate. Examine the examples below:

> *"Be quiet!" yelled Gramps.*
> *"Be quiet!" whispered Gramps.*
> *"Be quiet," chuckled Gramps.*
> *"Be quiet!" sniffled Gramps.*

To illustrate how differently a reader will imagine a scene based on the words that have been used, choose one of the previous examples and write a paragraph which uses that phrase. Compare your paragraph with some of your classmates' work to see the different scenes that have developed. As you make this comparison, remember that the key to writing the whole scene was in the verb that was chosen. It is only the verb that was changed in each sentence in the example.

_____

_____

_____

_____

_____

_____

Think about all the words you can use in your writing instead of *said*. Write as many as you can think of below. A few have been done for you.

laughed, cried, shouted _____

_____

_____

_____

Now write these words in the categories below. Some words can be used in more than one category. Can you think of other categories for your words?

Words to show happiness	Words to show sadness	Words to show excitement
laughed	cried	shouted
cried		cried
shouted		

On Your Own

The next time you write dialogue, read your piece aloud to a classmate. Ask him or her to count how many *saids* you used. Then ask him or her to help you think of more descriptive words to replace at least half of the *saids* in that dialogue.

LENDING A HAND TO "SAID"

Dialogue can be made much more interesting if the verb *said* receives some help from its partner, the adverb. Adverbs tell *how* someone "said" something. In addition, they give the reader more information about the character's feelings and the tone of the situation. Consider the example below.

> *"I wish I had a horse," said Celeste.*
> *"Me, too," said Sandi.*

Just adding adverbs makes a big difference and provides the reader with much more insight to the characters.

> *"I wish I had a horse," said Celeste wistfully.*
> *"Me, too," said Sandi sadly.*

Using words instead of *said* in combination with adverbs can make a conversation even more interesting.

> *"I wish I had a horse," sighed Celeste wistfully.*
> *"Me, too," agreed Sandi sadly.*

What are some of the reasons the third example is a better piece of writing? What does the reader learn about the situation or characters from this example that is not evident in the other two examples?

Choose one of the examples below and work with a partner to develop a one-page scene that you think goes with the tone expressed by the choice of verbs and adverbs. Share your creation with the class and notice how these small differences in words create a different picture in the reader's mind.

Choice #1: "I wish I had a horse," sighed Celeste wistfully.
　　　　　　"Me, too," agreed Sandi sadly.

Choice #2: "I wish *I* had a horse!" Celeste exclaimed angrily.
　　　　　　"Me, too!" Sandi added loudly.

Choice #3: "I wish I had a horse," cried Celeste desperately.
　　　　　　"Me, too," Sandi thought silently.

HAND IN HAND

You probably already know that it is impossible to write anything that makes sense without using nouns. You also probably remember that nouns include people, places, things, and ideas. Just for fun, try writing a paragraph without any nouns.

Here is a starter sentence: *While the ticked on, was running . . .*

When you finish, have a friend check to see that there are no nouns in your paragraph. Then read it aloud to the class and see how well they understand it.

Nouns, of course, must be included in your writing because they are what you are writing about. But nouns come alive when they are paired up with their partners, the adjectives. *Adjectives* are words that describe nouns. Consider the pairs below:

    blue sky   *mournful child*   *majestic horse*   *disgusting food*

Which word in each pair is the noun? Which word is the adjective?

Try this: Draw a picture of something, such as a dog, with only a pencil on white paper. Write as much as you can about this picture. Next, draw a second picture of the same thing. Add colors or other parts to the picture. Once again, write as much as you can about this picture. Which picture gives you more to write about? Why?

Adjectives are like the colors and additions you made to your second picture. They paint a more vivid scene for the reader. You might say that most nouns cannot live without their adjectives; they go hand in hand everywhere.

On Your Own

Expand the sentences below by adding adjectives to the nouns. Be creative and descriptive. Rewrite your sentences on the back of this sheet. Share your sentences with the class. Notice how the use of different adjectives changes the scene for the reader.

1. The snake slithered up the tree.
2. Under the porch lay a dog with a litter of puppies.
3. While eating an apple, the boy noticed a worm in it.
4. When the teacher walked into the room, all the children laughed.
5. The man climbed the stairs slowly to his room.

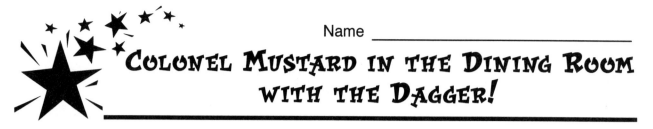

COLONEL MUSTARD IN THE DINING ROOM WITH THE DAGGER!

Your writing can become much more descriptive and interesting when you learn to use phrases known as *prepositional phrases*. Prepositional phrases usually tell where and when something is happening. A prepositional phrase begins with a word called a *preposition*.

Try this: When your teacher tells you to, move somewhere inside your classroom. Now tell your teacher where you are, and he or she will write what you say on the board. For example: "I am under the desk."

After all students have described where they are, underline the part of the sentence that tells "where." In the example above, "I am under the desk," *under the desk* tells where the person is. The preposition is the first word in each prepositional phrase, so in this example, *under* is the preposition.

Prepositional phrases can also tell when. Here is an example: During the movie, I ate popcorn and peanuts. What part of the sentence tells when? What is the first word of this phrase?

You can make prepositional phrases even more descriptive and informative by adding adjectives to the nouns in the phrases. Examples include "under the *large, blue* desk" or "during the *breathtaking* movie."

Here are some prepositions to help you create prepositional phrases in your own writing. Remember to use adjectives to describe the nouns in your phrases.

about	above	across	after	against	along	at
among	around	before	behind	below	beneath	by
between	down	during	except	for	from	in
inside	instead	into	like	near	of	off
on	onto	outside	over	past	since	to
toward	through	under	until	upon	with	up

Question: What are the prepositional phrases in the title at the top of this page?

_____

_____

On Your Own

Try writing a paragraph with at least one prepositional phrase in each sentence. You can experiment with using more than one phrase in a sentence, too!

EXPANDING A SENTENCE

Without some help, sentences can get pretty boring and dull. Words instead of *said* (verbs), adverbs, adjectives, and prepositional phrases help to spice up sentences and give them a life all their own.

Example: *The child cried.*
Under the old bridge, the lonely child cried softly into her teddy bear.

In this sentence, two prepositional phrases have been added: *under the old bridge* and *into her teddy bear.* *Old* and *lonely* were added to describe bridge and child. *Softly,* an adverb, was added to describe how the child cried.

The three-word sentences below really need some help. They have no "color" to them and provide very little information to the reader. Try expanding each sentence by adding at least one adverb, one adjective, and one prepositional phrase. You may add more than one, but be careful not to overdo it because too much spice is just as bad as no spice at all!

1. The dog barked.

   _____

2. The man yelled.

   _____

3. The girl laughed.

   _____

4. The glass fell.

   _____

5. The car crashed.

   _____

✍ On Your Own

Create your own three-word sentence like those above. Expand it as you did with the sentences above and then use it to begin a paragraph. Craft each sentence carefully, remembering to choose words that will paint the best picture for your reader.

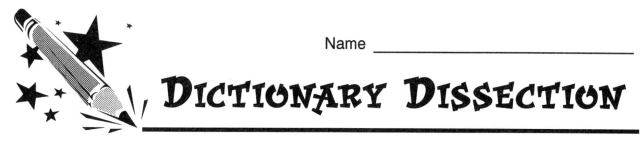

DICTIONARY DISSECTION

Most of us know that when we want to know what a word means, we can look it up in the dictionary. However, the dictionary can be useful in many other ways as well. Some dictionaries give several synonyms (words that mean the same) and/or antonyms (words that mean the opposite), as well as forms of the word, and definitions. To learn to use the dictionary more completely, here is an entry from the *Webster's New World Dictionary* to examine.

current (kur′ nt) adj. [< L. currere, to run] 1. now going on; of the present time 2. circulating 3. commonly accepted; prevalent —n. 1. a flow of water or air in a definite direction 2. a general tendency 3. the flow or rate of flow of electricity in a conductor —cur′rent•ly adv.

Can you read this entry? Try to answer the questions below.

1. Where in the entry is the pronunciation guide for the word? _____

2. In what ways can the word be used? (parts of speech) _____

3. From what language did the word come? _____

4. How is the original meaning of the word related to what it means today? _____

5. What other forms of the word are given? _____

6. What do *adj.* and *n.* stand for? _____

7. Why is the adj. definition given before the n. definition? _____

8. What are some synonyms for the word that can be found in the definitions? _____

   _____

What would you do if you did not know the answer to some of these questions? The answer (besides asking your teacher) is to look in the front of the dictionary in the section which is usually called "Guide to the Dictionary." This section explains the entries and how to understand each part of them. The dictionary is an important tool for a writer. Knowing how to use it to its fullest extent can make the writing process easier.

✍ On Your Own

Choose a word you would like to look up in the dictionary. Look it up and copy the entry exactly as it appears. Then develop five to ten questions about the word that can be answered from the entry. Exchange papers with a classmate and see if you can answer the questions by examining the dictionary entry.

RHYME TIME

Another type of dictionary that is often a necessity for writers is a rhyming dictionary. A rhyming dictionary lists words that rhyme according to the five vowel sounds. For example, suppose you had written a limerick poem whose first line was

Mr. Bill was a teacher so strict

and you could not think of anything to rhyme with *strict*. Using a rhyming dictionary, such as *The Capricorn Rhyming Dictionary*, you could look up "ICT" and you would find the following words listed:

addict, afflict, benedict, conflict, constrict, contradict, convict, depict, derelict, district, edict, evict, inflict, interdict, predict, relict, restrict, strict, verdict

Reading these words may very well help you develop the rest of the rhyme.

You can also add to this list by using "alphabet aid." Alphabet aid simply means that you start with "a" and write down all the words you can think of that rhyme with a certain word until you get to "z." When you use alphabet aid, you may find words that rhyme with the word you are using, but are not spelled in the same way. Here is an example of using alphabet aid with the word *strict*:

kicked, licked, nicked, picked, ticked

These words do rhyme with *strict*, even though they are spelled differently. Using a rhyming dictionary and alphabet aid can give you a wide variety of word choices to complete your rhymes.

On Your Own

Working with a classmate, select a word to find rhymes for. While you use alphabet aid, have your partner look the word up in a rhyming dictionary. Once you have all the words you can think of that rhyme with your word, make up a limerick or four-line poem that uses these words.

THESAURI

Of all the writer's tools, thesauri (plural of thesaurus) are probably the most valuable. A *thesaurus* is a book which contains synonyms (words that mean the same) and antonyms (words that mean the opposite) of words. While many words have similar meanings, in general, there are very subtle differences in their specific meanings. A thesaurus can be used to help a writer determine exactly what he or she wants to say in exactly the right way.

Try this: without looking in a dictionary, write definitions for the words below.

suitable   honest   desirable   agreeable   tasty

Do these words seem related to you in any way? In fact, if you look up the word *good* in a thesaurus, all of these words will be listed. That is because the word *good* in English has 14 different connotations. The *connotation* of a word is what the word means when it is used in a certain way.

Here are some sentences to go with the words above. See if you can match each word to the sentence that contains its connotation.

1. That man is a good man.   _____
2. This peach is good.   _____
3. The sun on my back is good.   _____
4. To win a lot of money is good.   _____
5. That hat looks good on you.   _____

✍ On Your Own

Look up these words in a thesaurus. Find at least five synonyms for each word. If antonyms are given, write several of them as well. After you have looked up each word, choose one of the words and write a sentence for each of its synonyms. Share your work with a classmate. Discuss the small differences between the synonyms and why you might choose to use a certain word in a sentence instead of another one.

bad   happy   sad   darkness   light

Name _____

ADDITIONAL AIDS

Many other reference books exist which assist the writer in the tough task of composing. Some of these include books of quotations, books on dialects (the way people speak in different parts of the country or world), books on specific kinds of words, books that explain the meanings and origins of sayings, or books about words used in a certain time period of history. These books often describe how and where the word began and the different ways it has been used through time. Reading about the origins of words and sayings can be fun and interesting. It can also give a writer ideas for topics to write about and ways to use a word or phrase.

Try this: Go to your library and see what books about words, phrases, or quotations are available. Find an interesting word, phrase, or quotation to share with your class. Write it below. Be certain to write down its origin and/or other noteworthy facts about it as well.

_____

_____

_____

_____

✍ On Your Own

Here are some words that have interesting histories and a variety of meanings. Find a book in your library that contains one of them and read about it. Report your findings to your class. You may even want to create an "Interesting Origins" bulletin board with the help of your teacher to record the word stories you discover.

dude   klutz   goat   turkey

Section 2

Poetry

WHAT IS POETRY?

What is poetry? This is a difficult question! Poetry has many forms and purposes. Before we explore some of the types of poetry, take a moment to think about poetry. Write your definition below.

Poetry is . . .

_____

_____

_____

Now think about what meaning poetry has for you. Do you enjoy rhyming stories? Do you like listening to songs? Do you create poems on your own to describe your experiences or feelings? Everyone has a different way of relating to poetry. Tell about ways you use or enjoy poetry below. Share your thoughts with some of your classmates.

To me, poetry means . . .

_____

_____

_____

Though each piece of poetry is very different, most poems have the following characteristics in common:

- They use language in a special way.
- They are usually written to convey a single experience.
- They are designed to bring out certain emotions in the reader.

For these reasons, words used in poems must be chosen very carefully. Because poems are much shorter than stories or novels, the author has less time to get his or her meaning across to the reader. This means that precise language must be used to ensure that the reader will understand the author's message. In addition, poetry is often designed to appeal strongly to one or more of our senses. That is why sensory language (words that help us see, hear, taste, touch, or smell) is very important. Look at the examples on the next page.

Talk with a partner about the images these words conjure up in your mind:

a sinister smile   a simple smile   a sweet smile

Now write a sentence to go with each phrase above. Notice how the precise use of adjectives makes a difference in the scene you create.

_____

_____

_____

Here are the beginnings to some poems which use the examples above. Choose one of them to finish.

A sinister smile had Aaron McGee
And I knew from the start, he was out to get me

It was a simple smile
and I held it in my heart

the sun
sent a sweet smile
to the orange grove below

_____

_____

_____

_____

_____

_____

_____

_____

POETRY IN MOTION

Have you ever heard anyone describe someone or something as "poetry in motion"? What do you think this phrase means? Write your ideas below.

_____

_____

_____

_____

People often describe movements they feel to be beautiful as "poetry in motion." Consider some of these examples:

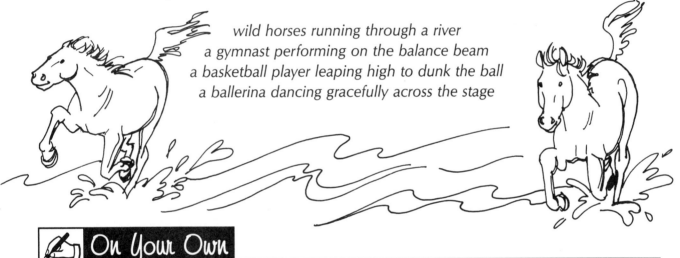

wild horses running through a river
a gymnast performing on the balance beam
a basketball player leaping high to dunk the ball
a ballerina dancing gracefully across the stage

On Your Own

Look through some magazines and find an example of something you consider to be poetry in motion. Paste this picture onto a piece of colored construction paper. Above, below, or around the picture, write words or phrases that describe the picture and your feelings about it. Believe it or not, you have just created a poem! Here is an example using the image of wild horses described above.

heads held high
tails out straight like arrows behind them
nostrils flaring
a collage of brown and black
red and white
splashing into the river
they run wild
they run free

COLOR POEMS

Capturing color is a great way to begin a poem. Colors have a great effect on us. They can help us feel happy or calm or excited. We associate many things, ideas, and feelings with certain colors. To begin your color poem, choose a piece of construction paper that is the color you want to write about. Take a few moments to look at the color. Then draw three circles on a separate piece of paper.

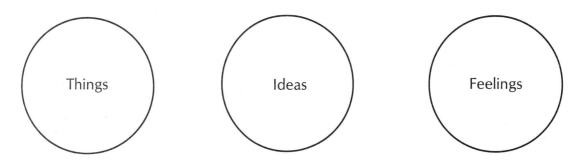

Now brainstorm in each category, listing all the things that remind you of this color. The example below may help get you started.

Once you have several items in each list, you can begin to organize them into a poem. Remember that your poem does not have to rhyme, but it may rhyme if you wish. You do not have to use everything from your brainstorm list. Here is a color poem using some of the items from the sample list above.

Brown is the color of my fine fast horse
the color of coffee
and of the strong, solid earth.

Brown is the color of my mother's lovely eyes
the color of my hair
and of gooey, gushy mud.

Brown is tender and warm
and soft and safe
Brown is like coming home.

BIOPOEM

Writing a biopoem is a wonderful way to share some things about your life. A biopoem is a snapshot of who you are. The formula for writing the biopoem appears below. After you write your biopoem, choose a classmate you do not know very well and exchange your biopoems. Then tell the class two new things you learned about him or her.

Line 1   Your first name
Line 2   Four traits that describe your character
Line 3   Relative (brother, sister, daughter, etc.) of _____
Line 4   Lover of _____ (list three things or people)
Line 5   Who feels _____ (three items)
Line 6   Who needs _____ (three items)
Line 7   Who fears _____ (three items)
Line 8   Who gives _____ (three items)
Line 9   Who would like to see _____ (three items)
Line 10   Resident of _____
Line 11   Your last name

Here is an example:

Ariela
Intelligent, caring, creative, observant
Daughter of Katherine and Kenneth
Lover of horses and unicorns and learning
Who feels sometimes lonely, sometimes happy, sometimes sad
Who needs open spaces and beauty and a morning cup of coffee
Who fears war and hate and brussel sprouts
Who gives knowledge, love, and time
Who would like to see world peace, Africa, and the end of poverty
Resident of California
Stein

I Used to Be, But Now . . .

The "I used to Be, But Now . . ." poem helps us think about the ways we have changed. Start by completing the chart below. First, list things about yourself that used to be true, but are not true anymore. Next, list things about yourself that have not changed. In the New Column, list things about you that are new.

USED TO BE	HAVE NOT CHANGED	NEW
a student like SpaghettiOs play Checkers have cats	a book lover horseback rider write poetry have freckles	play Scrabble have dogs a teacher drink coffee

Now use some of these items to write your poem. Here is an example:

I used to like SpaghettiOs,
but now I love coffee.
I used to play Checkers,
but now I play Scrabble.
I used to have cats,
but now I have dogs.
I used to be a student,
but now I am a teacher.
I used to be many things
that now I am not.
But I still write poetry,
like it, or not!

CONCRETE POEMS

These are not poems that are made from concrete! But they are poems that consist of images that you can actually see. The words of the concrete poem are arranged on the page to form a visual picture of the subject of the poem. For example, a poem about a tree would be written in the shape of a tree. A poem about a dog would be written in the shape of a dog.

To begin your concrete poem, choose a subject. Now think about words or phrases that describe how that subject looks (adjectives), what actions it makes (verbs), and what feelings it gives you. You can make lists or use circles like the ones below.

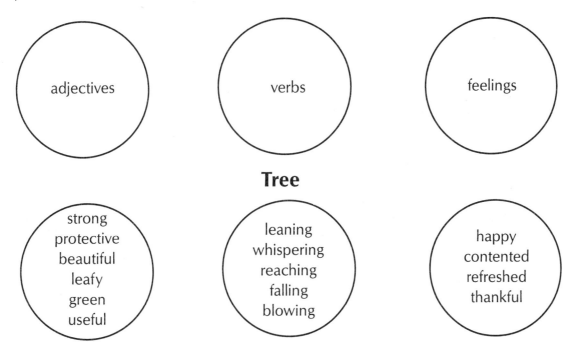

Tree

adjectives
verbs
feelings

strong
protective
beautiful
leafy
green
useful

leaning
whispering
reaching
falling
blowing

happy
contented
refreshed
thankful

Now write a poem about a tree, such as the one below. Next, arrange the words in the shape of a tree to form your concrete poem as shown on the next page.

Strong, protective, and beautiful
the tree whispers,
"Come."
"Come out of the rain."
It leans forward
branches reaching out
to gather me in.
I rest under its leaves,
grateful and content.

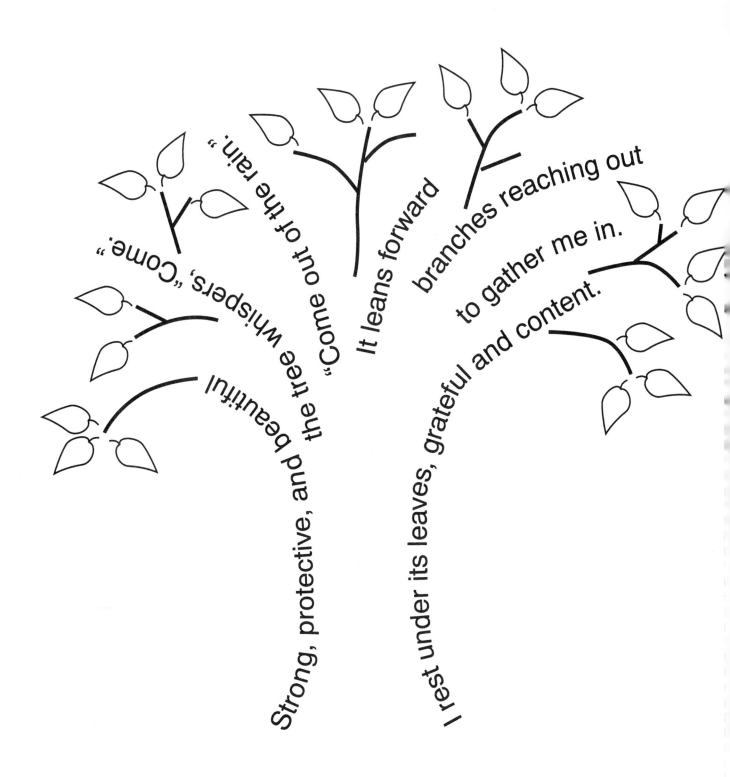

Strong, protective, and beautiful
the tree whispers, "Come."
"Come out of the rain."
It leans forward
branches reaching out
to gather me in.
I rest under its leaves, grateful and content.

DIAMANTE

The *diamante* is a poem that begins with one concept and gradually fades to the opposite idea. It has a strict form which results in a diamond-shaped poem. The "magic" of the diamante occurs in the fourth line, where the writer must begin the transition to the opposite idea. Word choice in this line is particularly important.

1 word

2 adjectives for word in line 1

3 participles for word in line 1

4 nouns—2 related to word in line 1, 2 related to word in line 7

3 participles for word in line 7

2 adjectives for word in line 7

1 word

(opposite)

A good way to begin your diamante is to choose the two opposite ideas before you begin writing the rest of the poem. As you form your poem, choose precise words. Avoid words such as *good*, *bad*, *big*, and *little*. Use a thesaurus to help you choose more descriptive words. The participles in lines three and five need to be words that end in *-ing* or *-ed*. Look at the example below and then try one on your own.

Dark
Peaceful, Cozy
Relaxing, Discovering, Understanding
Seawater, Night, Stars, Eyes
Laughing, Joking, Dancing
Alive, Brilliant
Light

CINQUAIN

A *cinquain (san kane)* is similar to a diamante because it has a specific form that must be followed and a certain number of lines. It is different, however, because it uses words that mean the same in its first and last lines (synonyms), rather than words that mean the opposite (antonyms). It is called a *cinquain* because *cinq* means "five" in French and a cinquain has five lines. A cinquain can be formed by using a certain number of words or syllables in each line. The general form is shown below.

Line 1: Word (title)   2 syllables or 1 word
Line 2: Description of word in line 1   4 syllables or 2 words
Line 3: Action describing word in line 1   6 syllables or 3 words
Line 4: Feeling about the word in line 1   8 syllables or 4 words
Line 5: Synonym for word in line 1   2 syllables or 1 word

A good way to start your cinquain is to choose the two synonyms before you begin writing the rest of the poem. Remember to choose words which really help the reader form pictures or feel emotions about your subject. A thesaurus is always helpful when doing this. Look at the examples below and then try one on your own.

Word Cinquains

Horse   Hunger
Majestic magician   Childhood menace
Flying through air   Stealing away life
A wonder of nature   Tragedy of our time
Friend   Death

Syllable Cinquains

Ocean   Roses
Lovely blue-green   Beautiful red
Singing soft lullabyes   Smelling like strong perfume
A special haven for us all   Love displayed in vibrant color
Blue sea   Beauty

HAIKU AND TANKA

These two forms of poetry come from Japan. Both have a strict style that relies on the number of syllables in each line of the poem. The subjects of haikus and tankas usually have to do with some aspect of nature and contain only a single thought about a special moment. Here are the formats for both types:

Haiku
a three-line poem of 17 syllables
Line 1: 5 syllables
Line 2: 7 syllables
Line 3: 5 syllables

Here are some examples of each type:

Haiku
The mist settles in
Covering the trees and moss
All the forest sleeps.

Life is so fragile
Delicate like a seashell
Drink in the beauty.

Tanka
a five-line poem of 31 syllables
Line 1: 5 syllables
Line 2: 7 syllables
Line 3: 5 syllables
Line 4: 7 syllables
Line 5: 7 syllables

Tanka
The foghorn bleats strong
Over and over it cries
Like a lonely lamb
Lost on a cold mountain ledge
Searching for its missing dam.

Wind in the tall tree
Whispering softly, calmly
Calling the beasts home
To rest in its lovely shade
To sleep in its canopy.

To begin your haiku or tanka, go outside and sit for a few minutes. Notice the sights and sounds around you. Focus on one of these and communicate your thoughts about your subject in your poem. Choose words that will help your reader feel as though he or she had been sitting beside you as you wrote.

LIMERICK

The *limerick* is a poem that is meant to be funny. That makes it an enjoyable poem to write. It has five lines and a particular rhyming pattern and rhythm. Lines one, two, and five rhyme and usually contain eight to ten syllables. Lines three and four have a different rhyme and only contain about five to six syllables. Here is an example:

Oh Pierce, gentle Equine Goliath	(9 syllables)
My patience you surely do tryeth	(9 syllables)
Though wisdom you lack	(5 syllables)
A fence you can crack	(5 syllables)
And the havoc you wreak makes me cryeth!	(10 syllables)

Notice the use of made-up words such as "tryeth" and "cryeth." A limerick is a good place to take "poetic license" with words, bending them into the shape you need to make them rhyme.

Limericks can also have several verses and become limerick stories or be sung to the tune of the "Limerick Song." Below is one such example.

Dr. Sharon, an equine physician
Found herself in an awkward position
With a finger quite broke
It could not even poke,
Much less make a proper incision.

An X-ray, however revealing,
To Sharon was not that appealing
So she just left it wrecked
Sighing, "Oh, what the heck."
While in pain all the while she was reeling.

Now Lori, her client and friend,
Said, "To this stuff, we must put an end
You shan't throw a stitch
You sassy old witch
'Till that finger you put on the mend!"

Work with a partner to write a limerick story of at least three verses. Read (or sing) your limerick to the class.

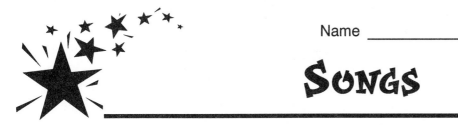

Name _____

Songs

Songs are poetry, too. Most everyone loves songs. The rhythmic beat and pleasing melodies of songs make them a special part of us. What are some of your favorite songs? Write their titles below.

_____

_____

_____

One of the reasons songs are enjoyed by so many people is because their words (called *lyrics*) speak to the listener. Sometimes, the words of a song can help people who do not write songs express their feelings.

Songs are usually written in verses with a chorus, or refrain. Most songs use end rhyme, which means the words at the end of the lines of the song rhyme in a certain pattern. The chorus is repeated or slightly changed as the song moves on. Like poems and stories, songs have themes. The theme is the message the songwriter is trying to convey to the listener through the song.

Listen to one of your favorite songs while you are looking at the lyrics. Then answer the following questions.

1. What is the song mostly about? _____

2. How does the song make you feel? _____

3. What do you think the theme of this song is? _____

4. How many verses does the song have? _____

5. Does the song use end rhyme? _____ If so, give an example from the song:

   _____

   _____

6. Does the song have a chorus? _____ How is the chorus different from the verses?

   _____

   _____

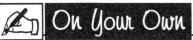 **On Your Own**

Now try writing the lyrics for a song of your own. It helps to have a tune, or melody, in your head when you do this. You can use a tune from a song you know to help you keep your lyrics in the right rhythm. Share your song with some friends.

Name _____

BALLADS

A *ballad* is a poem that tells a story. Often, this story is about adventure or romance and can easily be put to music. Ballads usually have four- to six-line stanzas that have regular rhythms and rhyme schemes. Many of them also have a refrain, which is similar to a chorus. Long ago, ballads were not written down, but passed to the next generation through song. Eventually, these stories were collected and recorded in writing for everyone to share.

Read the ballad on the next page and try to discover the story that is revealed in its stanzas. The questions below will help you.

Seaside Sailor

1. Who do you think is speaking in the poem? _____

   What words used in the poem lead you to believe this? _____

   _____

2. What do you learn about the speaker as you read the poem?_____

   _____

3. What do you learn about the "seaside sailor" as you read the poem? _____

   _____

4. In your own words, summarize the story told through this ballad: _____

   _____

   _____

   _____

5. Analyze this poem for the requirements of a ballad:

	Yes	No
Tells a story	____	____
Is about romance or adventure	____	____
Has stanzas of four to six lines	____	____
Has a refrain	____	____
Has a regular rhyme scheme	____	____

On Your Own

Find a ballad and bring it to class. Work with a partner to make up a melody for the poem and then sing it to your class, or write a ballad of your own and sing it!

Seaside Sailor
by Lorilynn

Seaside Sailor, lover of the sea
Who has sat beside you in the softly swirling breeze
Who has sensed your sadness, who has brought you joy
Seaside Sailor, no longer just a boy.

> What sweet dreams of reverie
> Swell inside your soul
> Silent sounds and memories
> Of ladies you have told
> I love you, Oh Mermaid of the Sea
> Climb aboard my ship and sail away with me.

Courageous Captain, keeper of the sail
Who have you pursued and loved to no avail
Who has sent you soaring, who has made you cry
Courageous Captain, whose spirit cannot die.

> What sweet dreams of reverie
> Swell inside your soul
> Silent sounds and memories
> Of ladies you have told
> I love you, Oh Mermaid of the Sea
> Climb aboard my ship and sail away with me.

Suntanned Skipper, dreamer of the past
Who now sits so near you, will her loving last
Who is caring deeply, who is reaching out
Suntanned Skipper, do you see what love's about?

> What sweet dreams of reverie
> Swell inside your soul
> Silent sounds and memories
> Of ladies you have told
> I love you, Oh Mermaid of the Sea
> Climb aboard my ship and sail away with me.

Name _____

FREE VERSE

Although there are no "rules" for writing this type of poetry, it is one of the hardest types to do well. Phrases must be worded carefully so that strong images are created. A good free verse poem uses many language tools to create its mood and its message. The poet must also be careful not to be too "sentencey," which means he or she must not write in a way that sounds like a paragraph instead of a poem. There is no regular rhyming pattern in free verse, and there may be no rhymes at all. Punctuation and capitalization rules may or may not be observed. The lines of the poem can be any length. A free verse poem appears on the next page. Read it and answer the questions below.

Prudence Island Morning

1. How does the physical organization of the poem help the reader "see" the images the poet is trying to create? _____

_____

2. Which of these writing tools do you see in the poem? Give an example of each one you find.

   simile _____

   metaphor_____

   personification _____

   alliteration _____

   onomatopoeia _____

   hyperbole _____

   symbol_____

   oxymoron _____

   rhyme _____

3. What senses (see, hear, feel, taste, smell) does the writer appeal to? Give examples of each one you find. _____

_____

_____

4. What is the poem about? _____

_____

5. What kind of feeling do you have for the subject of the poem? What words did the poet use to create that feeling? _____

_____

When you finish this activity, write a free verse poem of your own. Experiment and have fun!

PRUDENCE ISLAND MORNING

by Lorilynn

The night wavers
again
Like a silent cat
    padding
        into the forest,
it gradually retreats
from the heat
of the day

          The slow sun
            stalks
              stealthily
                after it
          Prodding the fog
          to
          fade and follow,
            splashing morning
          on the waves
            of the sea

The shimmering sailboat
stands silhouetted
against the still sky
the seagulls
    soar slowly above it,

Like a parent
          letting go
of a growing child's hand
the lighthouse light
relinquishes
its vigil

          A motor boat
            breaks a path
          across the bay
            Silence
          gives way
          to the gentle noise
          of a waking child

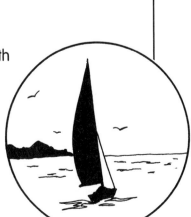

    the island
    begins to stir.

Section 3

"Shorts"

THE THIRD EYE

The "third eye" is the writer's eye. It is an objective part of yourself that you separate from the rest of yourself so that you can look at things in a certain way. It is the part of you that becomes another character so that you can see from that character's point of view. Read the example of this technique below and answer the questions that follow it.

She sat under the tree busily writing. After a few minutes, she paused, and as she looked up at the sky, the blond highlights in her brown hair caught the light of the sun. She must have enjoyed her summer, for her skin hosted a deep tan. The many freckles on her face had run together, giving the appearance of an even darker shade of brown. She seemed thoughtful and somehow melancholy sitting there so still. Suddenly, she returned to her work, as if an idea had just become clear. Watching her, I realized she must be a writer.

1. Which phrases tell about something the author can *actually* see from observing the person?

   _____

   _____

   _____

2. Which phrases show *guesses (or inferences)* that the author is making?

   _____

   _____

   _____

3. What is the "sum-up" sentence which shows the author is coming to a conclusion about this person? Is the sum-up sentence one which the author *knows* is true or one which the author is *guessing* to be true? Explain your answer.

   _____

   _____

On Your Own

Use your "third eye" to step outside yourself. Stand up and imagine that you have left your body in your seat. Now look at yourself from outside yourself, as though you were someone else looking at you. Describe what you see. Make certain that you ONLY describe what you see or what can be guessed from what you see. Be careful not to tell things about yourself that cannot be seen as you "sit" in your seat. Provide a "sum-up" sentence at the end of your paragraph based on what you have observed.

OBSERVING PEOPLE

Before you can create fictional characters, it is necessary to observe real people. Writers almost always use aspects of people they have known when developing their characters. This is because the characters will be more believable (seem more real) if they are modeled after real people. Becoming an effective writer means observing well. The little things about someone or something are often the details that bring the picture to life for the reader.

Observation is a two-step process. First, the writer takes notes on what he or she is observing. Later, those notes are woven into paragraphs. An example of this process is shown below.

Step 1: Notes: *Met on stairs—stout—polo shirt, white with red stars—red denim skirt—pearl earrings—gold bracelet, left arm—curly, short, almost black hair—red denim shoes to match skirt—diamond ring, yellow gold, ring finger left hand (probably married)—deft in movements on keyboard (implies experience)—early 40s.*

Step 2: Paragraph: *She smiled briefly as she climbed the steps and murmured a little "hello." She was dressed in a white polo shirt with bright red stars splashed about it. Her stout figure was encased in a red denim skirt and her feet bore shoes to match. She sat down at her desk and began her work. I watched the diamond sparkle of the ring on her left hand as she deftly maneuvered the keyboard. She seemed to be in her early forties and appeared quite comfortable with her job.*

It is important to note that not all the information in the notes needs to be used in the paragraph. As an author develops a character, he or she will often refer to these observation notes and may use some details later for further character development.

On Your Own

Choose someone to observe. You may want to choose someone who is working, playing, eating, sleeping, or doing some other activity. Take careful notes and develop them into a paragraph description later.

Be certain to include information which answers these questions: What is the person *doing?* How is the person doing the activity? What does the person *look like?* Does he or she have any *special features* like bushy eyebrows or a mole on the face? What is the person *wearing?* What kind of *attitude* does the person seem to have? How is the person *moving?* Is the person speaking? If so, *what* is he or she saying and *how* does he or she say it?

By doing this, you have created a character! Perhaps this character will appear in a story you will write in the future.

A Day in the Life ...

To get an idea of developing a character more completely, start by thinking about a typical day in your own life. This will help you provide details to your readers as your characters go about their business in your stories. Here are three different ways to begin such a description.

Scenario 1: (Character talking to self)
It's 5:30 a.m. There must be an air-raid siren blaring. No, wait a minute! It's that darn alarm clock! Can it be time to get up already?!

Gotta make the coffee. Gotta make the coffee. What day is this? Thursday? Yes. Oh, good, I can ride my horse this morning. I don't have to leave until 9:45. Wait, is it raining? No. Good. What's the time? 6:00. Coffee's done. Ah, sweet nectar of the morning!

Scenario 2: (Third person—as though someone was watching and writing)
She woke to the sound of an air raid. Instinctively, she pulled the covers back over her head and cowered under them moaning, "Not yet, I'm still too young!"

A hand reached over her and the noise abruptly ceased.

"Oh, there is a God! At least I have been given today!"

"That was the alarm clock, there, kid," her husband whispered sarcastically, "Wake up and smell the coffee."

Scenario 3: (First person—the author is telling the story)
My day begins with the sharp, electrifying cry of that lost Bird of Paradise, the modern alarm clock. More like an air-raid siren than anything else, but there is no escaping its message. Time to make the coffee. The day has begun.

On Your Own

Write about a day in your life. Experiment with ways to begin. Take the reader through each phase of your day, helping him or her to see, feel, hear, smell, and taste everything you do.

CREATING CHARACTERS

Characters are the people or animals that the story is about. Characters, like actors, can have major or minor parts in the story, but they are all important. Describing them so that the reader understands them well is a necessary task for a writer. Here is an example of a character description.

Emma Pearl looked at the muddy coffee in the bottom of her mug. **It has gone cold,** *she thought.* **So have I. Cold with the years.**

As she stared down at the cup, her eyes strayed to the worn knuckles, the bony fingers of the hands that knew so well the handle of the hoe, the feel of the plow. The torment of her life lay long in the shadow of her years. **Written on my hands. The suffering. Plain as day t'see.** *As if the callouses were a dot-to-dot puzzle and connecting them could unfold her history. Sitting there, following their map, she found herself reliving once again her painful past.*

In the passage above, the author uses the coffee mug and the woman's hands to set the tone of the piece. The coffee mug leads the reader to the hands, and the hands lead to the woman's thoughts. This helps the reader begin to "view" the character. The bold has been used to show the woman's *actual* thoughts. The author has not always used complete sentences. Why do you think this was done? What effect does it have on the reader? It is important to notice that the author did not actually tell things about the character but gave clues to the reader in the context of the story. Consider the difference by looking at the example of simply "telling" below:

Emma Pearl was an old woman. She was a farmer who had callouses on her hands from hard work. She had lived a painful life.

You will notice that it takes more words to give clues rather than tell about a character, but it is also much more interesting and effective.

On Your Own

Create a character of your own. Describe him/her/it so that the reader can see, feel, and understand—really have a sense for the character. Give your character something to do and describe him/her/it in that context. Your character description should allow the reader to answer the following questions:
- About how old is the character?
- What is the character feeling in this scene?
- What does the character look like physically?
- What is the character thinking at this time?
- What is the character doing right now?
- Do you feel you really understand this character from what has been written?

Observing Settings

When and where a story takes place are critical decisions for an author. Will it be a murder mystery at a lake? Will it be an adventure story in the mountains? Will it take place in a school, in the 1800s, on a ranch, in space?

Painting the scenery for the reader to see is a job a writer must take very seriously because the setting helps to shape the mood or feeling of the piece. Just like an artist, a writer needs to experience the scene he or she will write about to write it effectively. That is why many writers do research before writing certain stories or books. They often travel to places they wish to write about so that they can communicate the details of the setting and make the reader feel as though he or she is there.

Here is an example of setting description using the two-step process of observation (notes at the scene, write about it later).

Step 1: Notes: *late afternoon—sun hanging hot over the mountains—mountains cast in shadows with shades of green and blue—horses grazing in the foothills, swatting at flies—birds flitting about in the nearby trees—a far-off bark of a dog—no wind—strong smell of orange blossoms and jasmine fills the air*

Step 2: Paragraph: *As she walked toward her horse's stall, Adrienne drank in the strong sweet smell of orange blossoms and jasmine that filled the late afternoon air. She stopped for a moment watching the green and blue shadows on the mountains beyond. The sun, still hot, hung above them, as if placed there on purpose. She gazed out at the horses grazing in the foothills, lazily swatting at flies and listened to the birds darting about in the trees above her. Far off, she heard the bark of a dog at play. It was a beautiful place, this California.*

On Your Own

Choose a setting you would like to write about and go to that place or a place that is similar to it. (For example, if I wanted to write about Africa and I could not go to Africa, I might go to a zoo and observe African animals and their environment.) Spend some time there, paying close attention to what you hear, see, smell, taste, and feel. Take notes and then write a setting description later, using your notes.

Point of View

Did you ever stand on the top of a tall building or ride in an airplane and look out over a city? Did things look different from the way they looked when you were on the ground? The way a person sees something, whether that something is a city or a problem or a belief, is called *perspective* or *point of view*. Our point of view can change depending on where we "stand."

Try this: Write about the world from each of the places listed below. As you stand in each spot, look carefully at what you see and describe it well.

- a high place (such as a tree, tall building, airplane). Perhaps you could pretend to be a giraffe or large dinosaur and describe what you see.

- your own perspective—the way you see things from where you stand.

- a low place (such as lying in tall grass or in a hole or under a bench). Perhaps you could pretend to be an insect crawling through the grass or a rabbit scurrying about.

When an author decides how to present his or her story, a point of view must be chosen. What this means is that the author chooses the character or characters who will tell the story. Will the story be told using *I, he/she*, or will it be told from several characters' viewpoints? The most common points of view used in writing follow:

1. First person point of view—the narrator is a character in the story. The reader sees the story through this character's eyes only. This is when the pronoun *I* is used.

2. Third person point of view—the narrator is not a character in the story. The story is told from the perspective of one of the characters, but it is narrated from someone outside the story. This is when the pronouns *he, she, it* are used.

3. Omniscient (all knowing) point of view—the narrator is not a character in the story. The story is told from more than one character's perspective. Either first person or third person may be used when writing in an omniscient format. This is a difficult point of view to do well.

On Your Own

Choose one of the story ideas below and write an opening paragraph using the first person point of view—as though you were the character. Then write it a second time, using the third person point of view—as though you were watching someone.

a girl finds a lost puppy   a boy climbs a tall mountain

a man is trapped in an earthquake   a sled dog wins a long race

FLASHBACK

The *flashback* technique is an effective way of telling the reader about an event that happened at an earlier time. Some books are written entirely as flashbacks. This means that the character or narrator is not telling a story that is happening now, but is telling a story that happened in the past. Beginning a story with a flashback can present an interesting opening to a reader. Flashbacks may also occur at different times in a story and may happen inside a character's head.

We have all seen movies that use flashbacks. In movies, flashbacks can be shown without using words. Often, the director uses a different color of film or changes the music to indicate that a flashback is taking place. When writing a flashback, the author must do a similar thing with words. There must be clues that a flashback is occurring. Read the example below and identify the words that tell you the character is experiencing a flashback.

Rob gazed across the grassy meadow at the edge of the woods. It was quiet and peaceful. There was no sign of the tragedy that had taken place here last week. It almost seemed as if it had been a dream. He watched a moment more and then turned to go. Suddenly, a gunshot rang out. He saw again the majestic buck leap into the air and come crashing down. He heard the terrified scream of the wounded animal. No, he thought, not again! He whirled around to face the meadow, afraid of what he would find. But there was nothing there. He shook his head and looked again. Still nothing. Had what he'd heard been real? The meadow was undisturbed. The birds chirped happily in the nearby trees. Rob shook his head. As he turned homeward, he wondered if the memory of that horrible incident would ever leave him.

What words in this paragraph describe the actual flashback?

_____

_____

What words tell the reader that a flashback is about to occur?

_____

_____

What words tell the reader that the flashback is over?

_____

_____

Think of something you remember well that happened to you in the past. It could be something that happened a few minutes ago, yesterday, a year ago, or several years ago. Close your eyes and visualize the scene in your mind. Details are important. Try to bring as much detail into focus as you can. Then write down notes that answer the following questions.

Where were you? _____

_____

What things were around you? _____

_____

What sounds did you hear? _____

_____

Did you smell, taste, or touch anything? If so, what was it? _____

_____

What were you doing? _____

_____

What were you feeling? _____

_____

Why do you remember this incident? _____

_____

Now write a flashback for this event. You can write in first person, using I, or in third person, creating a character such as the one in the example. Remember to give the reader clues that a flashback is beginning and ending.

FORESHADOWING

Sometimes when we are reading a story, we suddenly get the feeling that something is about to happen, or will happen later on in the story. Often we can accurately predict what that "something" is. The reason for this is the use of a technique called *foreshadowing*. Foreshadowing occurs when the writer drops clues that something is going to happen. This creates a feeling of suspense or hopeful expectations in the reader and keeps the reader interested in reading on.

Movies use foreshadowing quite a lot. Unlike books, however, movies can foreshadow without the use of words. A change in music or the use of a different angle to shoot a scene can be enough to give us the clues that something is up. When writing a scene that uses foreshadowing, it can be helpful to visualize what that scene would look like as a movie and then capture it on paper.

Try this: Think of a movie you have seen in which something occurred that tipped you off about what would happen next or later on. On a separate piece of paper, describe the scene, giving clues about the event to come. Then hand your paper to a classmate and see if he or she can guess what will happen.

On Your Own

Write a prologue for one of the story titles in the box below. A *prologue* is an introduction. It is sometimes used to begin a story as a way of explaining about the story before the actual story begins. In your prologue, use the foreshadowing technique so that your reader will want to find out what is going to happen in the rest of the story. Here is an example from the prologue of the book *Tuck Everlasting* by Natalie Babbitt:

> One day at that time, not so very long ago, three things happened and at first there appeared to be no connection between them . . .

> No connection, you would agree. But things can come together in strange ways. But sometimes people find this out too late.

Murder on Mars	Journey to Egypt	Sarah's Trouble

DIALOGUE

Dialogue is the word used to describe a conversation between characters. Writing effective and interesting dialogue can be quite a challenge. Good dialogue needs to be appropriate to the situation in the story, realistic, and fit the character that has been created. There should also be a reason the author chooses to use dialogue. It needs to add something to the story, rather than be used to take up space. Here are two examples of dialogue. Work with a classmate to read them aloud. Then discuss which example seems more realistic—more like what Bill and his mother would actually say. Write down the reasons for your choice.

Both examples are meant to describe a conversation between Bill and his mom about a chore he did not complete.

Example 1

"Hey Bill," called Mrs. Talbot. *"What's up with that lawn mowing deal? I thought you were doing it today."*

"Naw, I don't feel like it. I'll do it tomorrow, Ma," replied Bill lazily.

"Okay, then, guess I won't make dinner either," said his mother angrily.

Example 2

"Bill," called Mrs. Talbot, *"would you come in here please?"*

Bill rose slowly from his chair and walked into the kitchen where his mother was busily cutting up potatoes for dinner.

"I thought you told me you were going to mow the lawn today."

"Oh, Mom, can I do it tomorrow? I just want to relax right now."

"No, Bill. Tomorrow you have baseball practice. You need to do it today."

"All right," Bill mumbled unhappily as he stomped out of the room.

On Your Own

Choose one of the situations below and write a conversation for it. Before you write, think of people you know and consider how they would talk in that situation. This will help you keep the dialogue realistic.

- two classmates on the playground talking about a birthday party they attended
- a father coaching his son at a sport
- a student in trouble with his/her teacher
- parents discussing where to go on a family vacation
- a group of children in a car pool on the way to school

DIALECT

Have you ever visited a part of the United States and wondered whether you had entered a new country because of the difference in the way people speak? Not only do accents differ in various parts of a country, but dialects differ, too. A *dialect* is the way people speak in a particular place. Using dialect when writing conversation can give more information to the reader about the characters, as well as make them seem more alive. Many times, dialect alone can tell your reader where the character is probably from, what race the character belongs to, the educational background of the character, or whether he or she is rich or poor.

Dialect is almost impossible to write well unless the author has had a good amount of exposure to that manner of speaking. Authors who wish to write authentic dialect may actually travel to the area where people speak the dialect to learn how to present it in their writing. Writers can also learn about dialect from people they know, from movies, or from reading books that use this technique or describe dialects from various parts of the world. Below is an example of dialect. After you read it, discuss with a classmate what you think you have learned about the characters from the dialect used.

   "Ya thinkin' 'bout Jack agin, ain't ya, Momma? Ya know, Momma," he began earnestly, *"sometime an apple goes bad. It weren't even wormy or nuthin'. Mebbe it jest had a wee bruise what festered. But it got t'be throwed out t'save the rest o' the bushel. D'ya hear what I'm sayin' t'ya, Momma?"* Kyle said softly. *"Sometime it got t'be throwed out."*
   "Even when it's throwed out, Kyle, sometime it leave a scar on the one next t'it. Mebbe not bad enuff to rot that one, but enuff t'make it fester, too. That's what done happened t'me and I wish t'the Lord that I could cut that bad spot outa my life and go on a livin'."

Notice that the use of dialect means that spelling, grammar, and word choice may not be in standard English form. A writer has to find a way to represent the sounds that are heard in a dialect. This means that he or she can break some of the usual rules we use when writing.

✍ On Your Own

Think of someone you have met or seen on TV or in the movies who speaks using a dialect. Write a conversation between yourself and this person. Use the dialect to give clues to your reader about the character. Here are some common dialects that you may have heard:

- London, England
- Southern U.S.
- Boston, Massachusetts
- Appalachian
- Dallas, Texas
- African American

COMPARE AND CONTRAST

Whether you are analyzing a story, writing an essay or poem, or creating characters, learning to compare and contrast are valuable skills. *To compare* means to show how things are alike or the same. *To contrast* means to show how things are different or not the same.

Words that show comparison

similar to	similar	have . . . in common	both
and . . . too	the same as	and either	be like
as . . . as	and so . . .	and neither	

Here are some comparison sentences using some of the words above.
1. *Both* Janet and Susan like horses.
2. I am going to college *and so* is Jessica.
3 Jake is not going swimming *and neither* am I!
4. Play-doh is *similar to* clay in many ways.
5. Heather loves to eat out, *and* Sheri does, *too*.

Words that show contrast

; however,	more than	less than	, but
different	different from	the most	-er than
on the contrary	the ____-est	; on the other hand,	

Here are some contrast sentences using some of the words above.
1. *On the contrary,* my dear, I love anchovies.
2. The bull is *stronger than* the mouse.
3. *The most* frightening sound is the loud clap of dangerous thunder.
4. I love quiet places; *on the other hand,* I also love crowds.
5. Daryl is very handsome, *but* he is not nice.

✍ On Your Own

Think of two characters who might be part of a story. In your first description of them, compare them (show how they are alike). In your second description, contrast them (show how they are different). Use the word lists on this page to help you show similarities (comparisons) and differences (contrasts). Share your work with your class.

CAUSE AND EFFECT

When something happens, it occurs because something else made it occur. For example, if you are placed on the Honor Roll, it is because you have received good grades. In this example, the *cause* of being on the Honor Roll was your good grades. The *effect* of your good grades was to be placed on the Honor Roll. Another way to say it follows.

I got on the Honor Roll *because* I got good grades.
Cause: good grades   **Effect:** got on Honor Roll

Another way to determine cause and effect is to ask the question "Why?"

Why did I get on the Honor Roll? Answer: Because I got good grades.
This means that your good grades were the *cause*.

To find the effect, ask: *What happened as a result* of my good grades? Answer: I got on the Honor Roll. This means that being placed on the Honor Roll was the *effect* (result) of receiving good grades.

Stories are made up of many cause-and-effect relationships. A character may stumble across a mystery *because* she finds an old map. Someone may die *because* they are lost in the wilderness. A ruler may lose his country *because* he is defeated in a war. An intergalactic mission may fail *because* it is ambushed by aliens.

On Your Own

Below are three effects. For each effect, write at least three possible causes. Then choose one of these cause-and-effect relationships and write a short story about it.

Effects		Causes
A wizard has lost his powers	because	_____
	because	_____
	because	_____
A puppy is found by a boy	because	_____
	because	_____
	because	_____
A girl is on a jungle adventure	because	_____
	because	_____
	because	_____

Sum It Up

When you "sum it up" in arithmetic, you add up all the numbers to find a total. This is similar to what you need to do when you summarize in writing. Composing an effective summary, however, is different from the arithmetic problem because you are not given the material you must add up. You have to decide what is important enough to be included in your summary. That is what makes summarizing difficult at times.

A helpful way to begin a summary is to think of the five Ws—*Who, What, When, Where,* and *Why*—and the question *How*. If you include information that answers these questions, you will have provided a good summary. Remember that a summary *does not include small details*. You only need to write about the main ideas that are necessary for a reader to understand what happened.

Summaries vary in their length and in the number of ideas presented. For example, if you are writing a brief summary for the back of a book cover, you will keep that summary to one or two paragraphs and you will not reveal the ending. If you are writing a summary for a book report, however, you might write one or two pages and you would reveal the ending. A complete summary of a book would include a brief description of the characters and the setting as well as all the main events in the plot.

> **Tip**
> When you begin to write your summary, start by listing the events or ideas *in the order in which they occurred*. Then use your list to create paragraphs that flow in a logical sequence.

On Your Own

Choose a book you have read recently. Make a list of the five Ws and how. First, write a one- to two-paragraph summary for the back cover of the book, which *does not* give away the ending. Second, write a more complete summary (one to two pages), which *does* explain the ending.

Who?
What?
When?
Where?
Why?

Section 4

True Stories

PERSONAL NARRATIVE

No matter what age you are, you have had experiences in your life that make interesting stories. You may have had a special friend who helped you through a hard time. You may have owned a pet who was unusual or meant a great deal to you. You may have had a frightening scare or an exciting adventure. You may have visited a place that you would like to write about. Things you like to do or do not like to do also make good subjects for personal narratives.

Personal narratives tell about your experiences. To write an effective personal narrative, you need to choose an experience that is memorable for some reason. An event that caused a strong emotional reaction in you will also make a good personal narrative. Keep in mind that personal narratives are fairly short and describe only one experience. Here is the beginning of a personal narrative:

I'll never forget my fifth grade teacher. She was a short, thin, German woman who had a good sense of humor and lots of energy. She took an interest in me and changed my life forever.

Miss Miller lived on a farm. It was a beautiful farm with many open fields. There was a humongous barn, an "L"-shaped barn like the kind you find only in the Midwest, and I loved to wander in it. There was a large farmhouse, too. It had two parts to it so two families could live there. I remember hunting for the ugly green tomato worms in her garden out back and squishing them dead by running a stick through them. We often went looking for bottles together along the roadside, turning them in for whatever they were worth at the time and then splurging at McDonald's, where I would always get a cheeseburger. But the time I remember best is when Miss Miller taught me how to shoot the pesky sparrows that bothered the barn. It was the first time I ever took an animal's life, and the last.

On Your Own

Begin your personal narrative by brainstorming ideas. Some categories that may be helpful are
- memorable friends or pets
- special vacations or trips
- people who have been important to you
- an event that made you feel very good/bad/sad/angry/surprised
- an event that helped you learn an important lesson
- things you like/do not like to do

When writing your personal narrative, remember to use descriptions that help the reader see, hear, feel, smell, or taste what is going on. Techniques such as foreshadowing and dialogue can also bring life to writing. Be certain to include your thoughts and feelings as well, so the reader can identify with what you experienced.

AUTOBIOGRAPHY

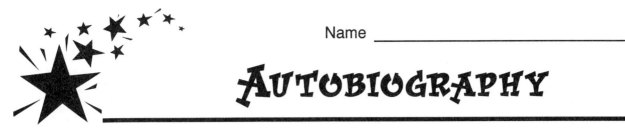

Writing about your life can be fun as well as give you a better understanding of your own history. An *autobiography* is the story of your life that you write yourself. When you write your autobiography, you can tell the entire story of your life or only part of it. You can make a long book with different chapters, or you can put down the main events in a story. However you choose to write it, your autobiography needs to be interesting and descriptive, taking your reader through the journey of your life. Consider the two examples below:

Example 1: *I was born on April 2, 1984. I was the first child. We lived in Malibu, California, in a large house. My parents were happy to have a daughter at last.*

Example 2: *My parents tell me it was quite a happy day when they brought me, their first child, home from the hospital. Of course, I don't remember, but I should think it* was *a happy day. After all, it was me they were bringing home!*

What are some of the differences in the writing styles of the two examples?

_____

_____

_____

Which example do you find more interesting? _____

Why? _____

_____

_____

What do you learn about the writer's character in the second example that you do not learn in the first example? What words help you understand this?

_____

_____

_____

Before you begin writing your autobiography, think about what you will include in it. Here are some categories to help you get started. Once you have brainstormed in these categories, you can start to write the story of your life. When you are finished, share it with your classmates.

Earliest Memories   Major Influences   Biographical Facts
Important Events   Important People   Family Facts
                           Major Accomplishments   Memorable Pets

BIOGRAPHY

Biographies are a form of nonfiction writing that tell the story of another person's life. Biographies require the author to do some research on the person he or she is writing about. Although biographies are often written about famous people, you can write a biography about anyone. Choosing to write about someone in your family, or extended family, can be an opportunity to get to know that person better.

Interviews are an important part of gathering information for a biography. Tape recording the person's answers and taking good notes are ways to keep track of your subject's answers, comments, and stories about his or her life. When creating your interview questions, you will need to do the following:

- Before you begin writing your questions, make a list of what you already know about this person.
- Avoid writing questions that can be answered "yes" or "no" because these answers give you very little information.
- Think about how this person might respond to your questions and create follow-up questions to ask to get a better picture.
- Make certain to get a few anecdotes (a short story about an interesting, amusing, or strange event) from your subject to include in your biography.

On Your Own

Choose someone you know that you would like to know more about. Create at least 20 interview questions to help you research this person's life. Some examples are listed below.

1. When and where were you born? Was there anything unusual or noteworthy about your birth?
2. How many brothers and sisters do you have? Describe them. Were you especially close to any of them?
3. Where did you live the first five years of your life? What memories, if any, do you have of this time period?
4. What do you remember about starting school? Where did you go to school at this time?
5. Did you move during your childhood? If so, when and where did you move? How did you feel about these moves, and how did they affect you?
6. What do you remember about your elementary school years (ages 5-11)? Did you have any special experiences or friends during that time? Were there any significant adults, other than your parents, who influenced you? If so, tell about these people and how they made a difference in your life.

Anecdotes

A short story about an amusing, interesting, or strange event in a person's life is called an *anecdote*. Anecdotes can add a great deal to writing, whether the piece is fiction or nonfiction. They help the reader have a better understanding of a character and the events in that character's life. Sometimes an entire tale can be made up of a series of anecdotes. Here is an example:

When I was about 14, I worked for a neighbor taking care of his horses. In the barn, the stairs to the hayloft were inside one of the stalls. There was a door that separated the stall from the stairs, but it only had a simple latch to keep it locked. The horse who called that stall home was a big, red gelding whose name was Sonny. I remember being a little concerned that Sonny might get that door open someday, but I didn't really think it would be a problem because there was a 90-degree turn in the stairs, and who ever heard of a horse climbing stairs, anyway?

One day, however, I arrived at the barn only to find Sonny standing in the hayloft. I could not believe my eyes! How were we going to get him down? For a week we tried coaxing him down the stairs, but no luck. Finally, the owners piled bales of hay in a ramp-like shape from the ground to the outside hayloft door. A veterinarian came and tranquilized Sonny, and a few strong men literally rolled him down the hay ramp to the ground below. Safe and sound, and no worse for wear after his experience, Sonny awoke and resumed his horsey behaviors. After that, though, the stall was shortened so that the door to the hayloft was on the outside!

On Your Own

Make a list or brainstorm some experiences that have happened to you that have been very funny, unusual, or extremely interesting. Choose one of these to write as an anecdote. Perhaps you can use this anecdote for a character in a story or as part of your own autobiography.

When the roller coaster got stuck upside down

How I was chased by a bear

The time my mother locked her keys and the baby in the car

SONNY

CHARACTER SKETCH

A *character sketch* is a description of an actual person. It is more than just a physical description, however. A character sketch is designed to give the reader insight about the person and includes the way the person thinks or feels, how the person views life, and/or what philosophy the person may have. Usually, the writer tries to present the character in a certain way so that the reader will have a specific response to that person. Rather than just telling the reader what the character looks like, the physical description of the character is woven into the writing at different points. It is a little like connecting a dot-to-dot puzzle—slowly the reader begins to form a picture of the character and an understanding of this person's personality. To help you get an idea of how to write a character sketch, read the sketch below and answer the questions that follow.

Jasmine Principle was not just anybody. From the moment she walked into the room, you knew you could not escape her. Her sharp, black eyes darted about constantly, taking in everything that was going on. Sure, you could try to pass a note or whisper to your friend, but ol' Miz Principle would catch you and you'd do time. Detention time, that is.

Every day, Miz Principle would enter the classroom in a different way. You never knew if she would tiptoe in quietly, rush in on roller skates, or stomp in wearing army boots. Her auburn curls boasted a new style daily, too—sometimes rolling down her back, sometimes wrapped in a bun or cranked into a tight ponytail, and occasionally looking much like a ratty old bird's nest. On those days, we were sure she'd just forgotten to brush it. She was kind of forgetful. A little batty, we'd sometimes say. But then, she was pretty darn old, too. And old people usually are a little batty.

One thing that was true about Miz Principle, though, was that she was one heck of a good teacher. She made sure you really knew stuff. I mean, she didn't just teach it and move on; she required you to show her you could use what she'd taught you.

1. List all the physical characteristics that the author has revealed about Miz Principle.

   _____

   _____

2. List all the aspects of Miz Principle's personality—clues to the type of person she is—that have been given or suggested.

   _____

   _____

3. From the way the author has written this piece, how would you say he or she wants the reader to feel about Miz Principle?

_____

_____

4. When a character sketch is well done, the reader can "see" the character in his or her mind and predict how the character will probably behave in a certain situation. Try this with Miz Principle. Draw a picture of her. Share it with your classmates and compare their pictures to see how many elements are the same. Then write a paragraph predicting how Miz Principle would respond to one of these situations:

   • a spitwad being thrown at her
   • a student who could not use a ruler correctly
   • a child who dyed his hair purple and green

Once again, compare your ideas with those of your classmates. Discuss the reasons you made Miz Principle act in a certain way in your writing.

On Your Own

Think of someone you know well that can be used for a character sketch. List this person's physical characteristics and the elements of his or her personality. Decide how you feel about the person and how you want your reader to feel about him/her. Remember that a character sketch is like a portrait, so details are important.

REAL-LIFE DRAMA

Drama is another word for a story that is told by actors, commonly known as a play. You can take any real-life story, such as a biography, autobiography, adventure, mystery, or love story and write it as a play. When writing a play, however, you have to add something to your writing that is not necessary in other forms of writing. These are *stage directions*. Stage directions set the scenes and tell the actors what to do or how to say their lines. Stage directions appear in parentheses and are not meant to be said out loud. Here are some examples:

ACT I, SCENE i
(The great ship has just docked at the pier.
BRANDON and ALISA are standing on the pier
with their suitcases. MOTHER is behind them, weeping.)

MOTHER: (dabbing her eyes with a handkerchief) Goodbye dears. God keep you.
BRANDON: (hugging her) Goodbye, Mama.
ALISA: (between sobs) Why can't you come with us, Mama? I can't go without you.

Some important points to remember when writing your play are listed below:
- Acts are like chapters in a book.
- Scenes usually change when the setting of the play changes.
- Realistic dialogue is very important because the characters are telling the story to the audience.
- Dialogue does not have to be in quotation marks because the character who is speaking is identified at the beginning of each speaking part.
- Remember to visualize your play on stage and write clear stage directions when necessary.

On Your Own

Choose a real-life story that you have been involved in that would make an interesting play. Maybe you were on a camping trip when something exciting or unexpected happened. Maybe you had an unusual adventure or solved a mystery of some kind. Decide which people from your experience should be characters in the play, and what the major settings (scenes) of the play should look like. Before you begin, write down some details about the characters and the setting. You also need to set up the main problem early in the play, so that the characters can go about solving it as the play unfolds. Most plays communicate a message or lesson about life which is portrayed through the actors' words and actions. Decide what message you want to send through your play. It may be a lesson that you, or someone who was with you, learned as part of the experience. As you complete your play, do not forget to show how things finally worked out.

SPEECHES

Speeches are an opportunity for you to inform others about a topic and/or persuade them to view things in a certain way. We often think of speeches when we think of people running for political office such as the presidency. Political speeches are only one type of speech, however. Any time a person must speak in front of a group, he or she must prepare a speech. A graduation speaker needs a speech, a minister needs a speech, a person narrating a slide show needs a speech, and a person who is speaking at a conference or meeting needs a speech.

Effective speeches, like all pieces of writing, require careful choice of words. The purpose of the speech must be clear. Are you trying to encourage people to vote for you? Are you trying to help people see the importance of saving the whales? Are you trying to inspire people to reach new goals? Are you trying to explain a topic you have researched? These are important considerations that must be decided before you write your speech.

Once you have your purpose in mind, you can build your speech around it. Some ingredients you may need to include in your speech are examples, reasons, steps, important statistics, a series of questions, a short history, or anecdotes.

Remember that speeches are meant to be heard, so they must *sound* good as well as be well written.

Here are some tips to remember when writing your speech:
- **Think** about who your audience will be and write your speech so that *this* audience will understand it. Avoid words or ideas that may not be understood by this audience.
- **Consider** how long your speech should be. This may be partly determined by your audience and partly determined by the subject of your speech.
- **Avoid** "wordiness." Say what you need to say in a direct and effective way and be done with it.
- **Before** you begin, read or listen to several different kinds of speeches so that you have an idea about how to proceed.
- **End** by restating the purpose of your speech and emphasizing the importance of what you have said.

✍ On Your Own

Choose a topic for a speech. Create a "speech" map like the one on the next page. Once you have your map, you can begin to fill in the "scenery" (the details and language) that rounds out your speech.

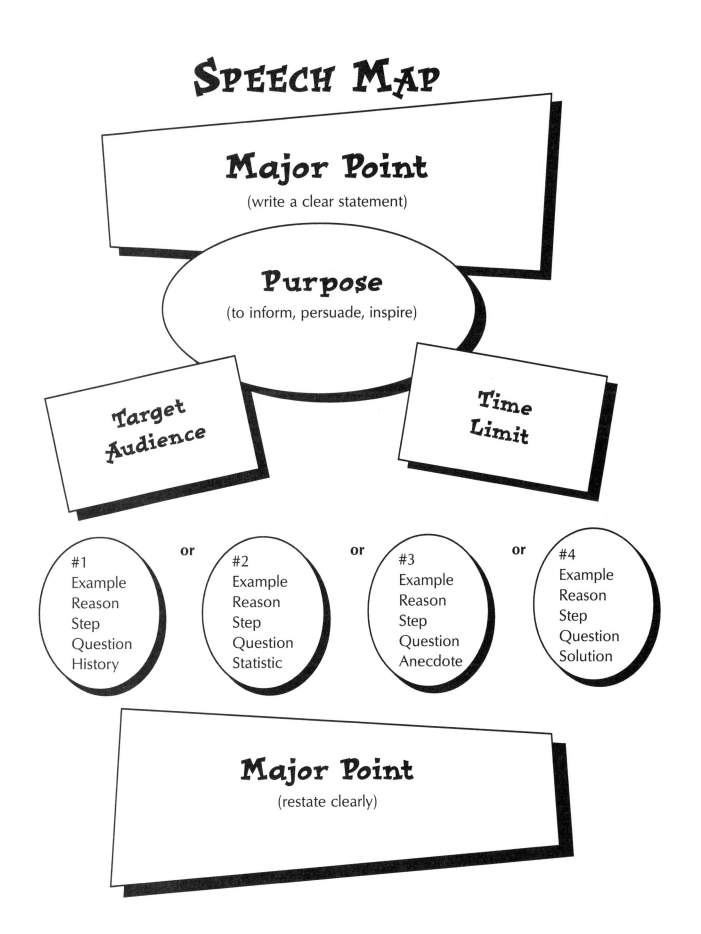

SPEECH MAP

Major Point
(write a clear statement)

Purpose
(to inform, persuade, inspire)

Target Audience

Time Limit

#1
Example
Reason
Step
Question
History

or

#2
Example
Reason
Step
Question
Statistic

or

#3
Example
Reason
Step
Question
Anecdote

or

#4
Example
Reason
Step
Question
Solution

Major Point
(restate clearly)

Essays

Just like a speech, an essay must have a main point. And like a story, it must also have a beginning, a middle, and an end. Two types of essays that are interesting to write are the informative essay and the persuasive essay. The informative essay presents information to the reader. The persuasive essay tries to get the reader to agree with the author's point of view. Both types of essays follow the same general format. Here are some guidelines for writing essays:

Begin by writing a sentence that states the main idea of your essay. This statement is called the *thesis*. Here are two examples of thesis statements:

Informative: The Mexican wolf is a rare and interesting animal.
Persuasive: Without careful plans to preserve the Mexican wolf, it will soon become extinct.

Introduction

Next, begin the introduction by capturing the reader's interest in some unique way. **Introductions** have two basic parts. **The first part** of the introduction, contains five to ten sentences which provide general background information on the topic to help prepare the reader's mind for the subject. There may even be two paragraphs to the introduction, as shown in the first example found in the Appendix. **The second part** of the introduction is the very last sentence in the opening paragraph and this is where you write your thesis. **The thesis states the reason the paper is being written.**

Thesis

Body

Now you are ready to write the body of your essay. The *body* contains subtopics that relate to or support your thesis. In the **informative** example above, the body might contain subtopics like the Mexican wolf's coloring, its habitat, and its reproduction. The body of the **persuasive** essay might have subtopics, such as statistics, reasons the wolf has become endangered, and plans to preserve the wolf. The body is the longest part of your essay.

Restate Thesis

Conclusion

Lastly, your essay must have a conclusion. Conclusions, like introductions, have two basic parts. The first part restates the thesis (the main idea) in slightly different words. The second part contains five to ten sentences that sum up what was said in the body of the essay, returns to the bigger idea with which the introduction began, and predicts what might happen in the future. Conclusions should continue the writing style that was used in the introduction.

Essays can be written in many different ways. They can begin like a story. They can start by stating background information about the specific topic. Or they can open by giving background information about the broader topic related to the essay. In the Appendix, you will find examples of all three ways to begin a persuasive essay on the endangered species, the Mexican wolf. Each one uses a different approach, but all three provide the background information necessary to get the reader's mind ready to learn more about the topic. You may choose any of these ways to begin your essay, but the style you choose to begin the essay must also be the style you use to end the essay when you write your conclusion. To assist you, the appendix also contains the conclusions for each style of introduction.

On Your Own

Decide whether you want to write an informative essay or a persuasive essay. For an informative essay, you can choose most any topic. For a persuasive essay, however, your topic should be something you feel strongly about. Remember that you will be trying to convince people to believe as you do in this essay, so you need to have solid reasons behind your opinion.

Name _____

HEADLINE NEWS

There are many types of newspaper articles that can be written. The basic requirement of a newspaper story is that it concerns something that is happening in the world today. Writing news stories gives you a chance to be a reporter, to collect data about an event or problem of interest, and to pass it along to readers.

ONE: Start by reading through a newspaper and answering the following questions:
1. What types of stories are *front page news?* Why do you think these stories are chosen for the front page?
2. What are the different sections in the newspaper and what are they used for?
3. What is the function of the *headline* in an article?
4. What is important about the first paragraph (called the *lead)* in an article?

TWO: Choose one article to read and answer these questions about it:

Who is it about?_____

Who would want to read it?_____

What is it about? _____

When did it occur? _____

Where did it occur? _____

Why did it occur? _____

How did it occur? _____

How will the reader benefit from reading this article? _____

THREE: Work with a partner to examine these three types of stories found in a newspaper and make a chart similar to the one below to record your findings.

Type of Story	Similarities	Differences
News		
Human interest		
Editorial		

✍ On Your Own

Choose one of the types of stories above and write an article for your local newspaper. Remember to write about something of interest to your community and to get the facts from a reliable source. Create an eye-catching headline and an interesting lead for your story. When you write the ending, be certain to leave the reader with something to think about.

BOOK REPORT/REVIEW

Writing a book report and writing a book review are very similar tasks. For both the book report and the book review, the following elements must be present:

Plot: This is the series of related actions or events in the story in the order in which they occurred.

Conflict: This is the struggle between opposing forces in the story (such as good and evil) or a problem that must be solved.

Resolution: This is the way the struggle is ended, the way the problem is solved, or the way the story comes to a close. If there is no resolution, the struggle may not have ended, the problem may not be solved. Sometimes this does happen.

Climax: This is the point of highest interest or excitement in the story. It is often described as the *turning point* in the story because things are usually different in some way after the climax has occurred. The climax usually occurs near the end of the story.

Characters: These are the people, and sometimes the animals, who take part in the story's events.

Setting: This includes the place(s) and time period in which the story is happening.

Theme(s): This is the general idea(s) about life that a story communicates, the message(s) of the story. If you ask yourself, *why did the author write this book,* you will probably find the theme in the answer to that question.

Coming Full Circle: Usually, a story comes back to the beginning in some way, either through the setting or by the action of the characters. If you watch a movie carefully, you will see that this is done in films as well. Often, the movie opens and closes in the same place as it began. This gives the reader or viewer a feeling of closure, which is important when a story ends.

The critical difference when writing a book review is that the writer offers an opinion of the book he or she has read. The author must also give reasons for his or her opinion and may often quote examples from the book. You can find examples of book reviews in both newspapers and magazines.

On Your Own

Write a book report or book review about a book you read recently. If you choose to write a book report, look in the Appendix of this book for some more guidelines. If you choose to write a book review, cut out two book reviews from newspapers or magazines, read them first, and attach them to your book review.

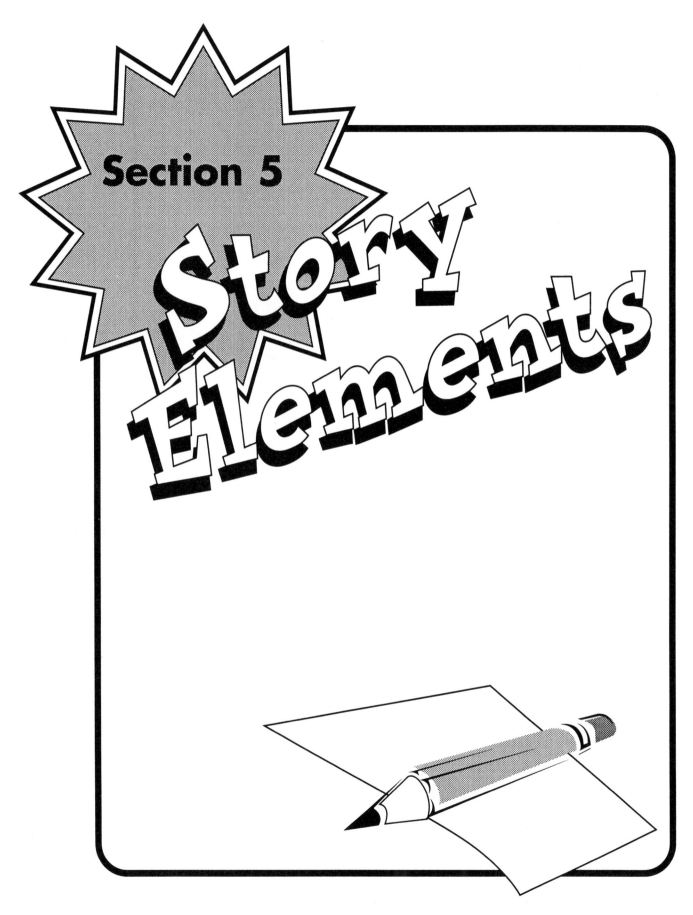

Section 5

Story Elements

WHAT TO WRITE

This is always the question! There are two cardinal rules of writing to be followed when choosing a story topic:

One: **READ** several books that are similar to the type of story you wish to write.
Two: **WRITE** about something you know well, or something that really interests or excites you.

When writing fiction, your imagination can fly free, but you still need to create a story that makes sense. Even if the story is a fantasy, a dream, or takes place in the future, your readers must be able to believe in the story and to stay with the ideas you are presenting.

There are several ways to begin gathering some ideas for your story. One way is to think about **what type** of story you might like to write. Here are some kinds of fiction stories:

fantasy   myths   mystery   adventure

legends   realistic fiction   sports

historical fiction   plays   animal stories

Another way is to brainstorm topics you know well or are of interest to you.

horses   rock climbing   Grand Canyon   song writing

solving a crime   discovering a new planet

A third way is to make an idea web. Choose a topic that interests you and brainstorm ideas related to that topic. Each line in the diagram below shows where the writer's thoughts traveled from one idea about dogs to another.

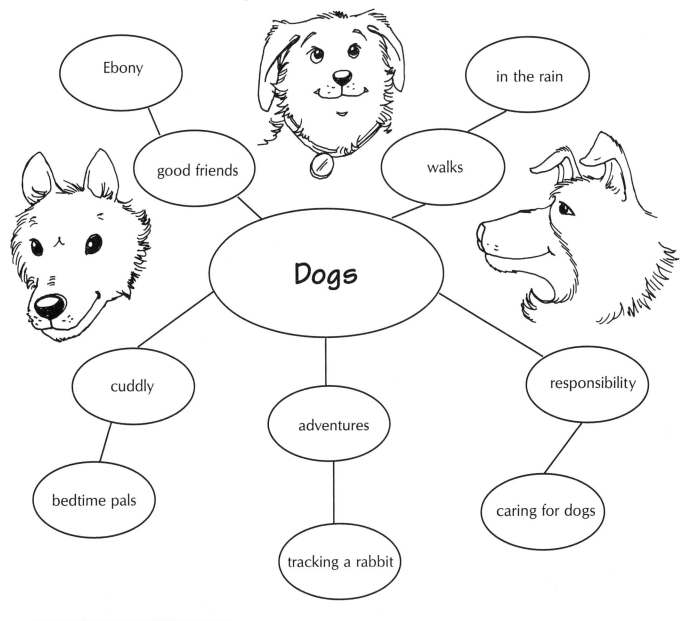

GOOD AND EVIL

You have probably read many stories that had a "good" character and an "evil" character. Usually, these two characters are working against each other, trying to get their own way, win a war, or somehow eliminate the other person. There are special names for these main characters:

Protagonist: the "good" character. This character is usually the one with which the reader can sympathize or learn to understand. It is the character that the reader wants to see "win" or come out on top in some way.

Antagonist: the "bad" character. This character is usually the one that the reader does not like. It is the character that the reader wants to see "lose" or "get what he or she deserves."

The protagonist and the antagonist are *very* important characters. The struggle between them (called the conflict) is what makes the story interesting.

On Your Own

Once you have an idea for a story, think about who the protagonist and the antagonist will be. After you have chosen the basic characters, use the webbing technique to create a "picture" of each character. An example appears below:

has a beard and moustache

has red hair

has front gold tooth

has mossy teeth

Antagonist: Pirate

smokes cigars

laughs in a menacing way

has a pet python

CONFLICT AND RESOLUTION

In every story, there is a problem of some kind. This is known as *the conflict.* The conflict may be between two characters, between groups of people, between a person and the environment, between a person and an unknown force, or even between the person and him or herself. There must be some kind of conflict, however, or the story will not be very appealing.

Stories must also have a *resolution.* A resolution is a solution to the conflict. Some examples of resolutions might include good winning over evil, a person outlasting a harsh environment, or a journey coming to an end. Without a resolution, the reader feels dissatisfied and is often unhappy with the story.

Your main character (protagonist) should have some kind of goal in your story. Maybe she has to solve a crime or is searching for her lost parents or is surviving a plane crash in the mountains. The conflict develops because the character is unable to reach this goal right away. You, the writer, put something in her way (the antagonist)—something that she must overcome, outsmart, or do away with. *How* she overcomes this obstacle results in the resolution to the problem.

On Your Own

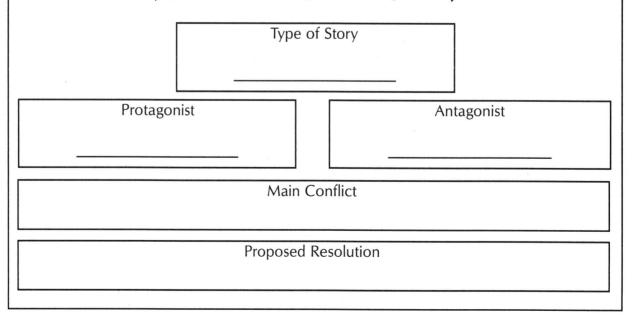

Using the skeleton map below, sketch in an outline for a story. These are basic idea boxes and you may decide to change them as you write. Once you have your map, take some time to develop your characters using the webbing technique.

Type of Story

_____

Protagonist

_____

Antagonist

_____

Main Conflict

Proposed Resolution

PLOT

The *plot* of a story is the sequence of events that happens as the story unfolds. In the beginning of the story, the writer must explain anything that took place before the story begins, describe the setting, and introduce the characters. After this, the conflict slowly takes shape. Events occur that lead the main character(s) to a problem, a climax (the most exciting part or the turning point in the story), and a resolution. A diagram of a plot appears below:

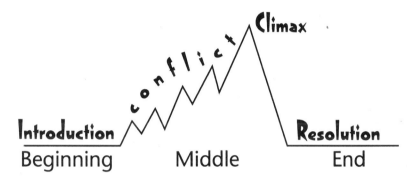

The real trick about all of this is to continue the problem for a while in an interesting way before a resolution occurs. To keep the reader engaged, it is very important to block the main character from reaching his/her goal or solving the problem too quickly. In the diagram above, the character was blocked four times. This is shown by the low points in the conflict line as the story climbs toward the climax. The first block is marked with an asterisk.

Once you have made your introduction, set up the problem, and blocked the character from solving the problem a number of times, you can conclude the plot by creating the climax and writing the resolution. Before you do that, however, spend some time thinking about how to block your character. Below are some problems you might find in a story. Think of at least three ways to block each character before allowing him or her to reach the goal.

Problem #1: Tyrone is trapped by a fallen beam in an earthquake. He must free himself.

Problem #2: Elana's best friend has stolen some make-up from a store. Elana must decide what to do about this crime.

On Your Own

Write two problems a story might have. Exchange papers with a classmate and create three to five blocks each character must overcome before he or she can resolve the problem. When you are both finished, discuss your ideas and decide which one of the plots would make the best story. Give two reasons for your choice.

CLIMAX

When you are watching a movie and the most exciting part is about to happen, there is usually a special signal that tells you something *very* important is coming up. Do you know what that signal is? It is music. Music lets the audience know that the climax is approaching. The *climax* is the highest point of interest or suspense. It is also the turning point in the story. This means that the excitement is no longer building; it has reached its peak. The problem is now solved. The climax comes quite near the end of the story. After it, the story will soon end.

The difficult part about "orchestrating" a climax in writing, rather than in a movie, is that there is no music. The author must create the "music" so that the reader will hear that suspenseful tune in his/her head and realize that the climax is about to occur. To do this well, you will need to choose your words carefully. Remember that you are both the eyes and the ears of your readers and you can only lead them to the climax through the words you write.

Below are two examples of a climax. Which one do you think provides a better picture for the reader? In the example you choose, circle the words you feel are the most effective in creating an exciting scene.

Example 1: The canoe sped rapidly down the swiftly moving river toward the dangerous falls. Jake and Alicia paddled frantically, but could not steer the boat. It plunged on and time was running out. Alicia's eyes were wild with fear and her voice seemed to have vanished. The thundering sound of the waterfall ahead pounded in her ears. Jake shouted at her to try once more to turn the canoe toward the shore, but she did not respond. Suddenly, Jake saw a low hanging tree branch ahead. Quickly he grabbed the rope in the bottom of the boat and tied it through the front of the canoe. Then he made a lasso at the other end. As the canoe drew closer to the branch, he swung the rope, sending the lasso over the end of the protruding limb. The canoe halted with a violent snap as it hit the end of the rope. Jake knew it would not hold for long. He grabbed Alicia and boosted her up into the tree. Then he hauled himself up as well. They were safe at last.

Example 2: The canoe was moving very fast. Soon it would reach the falls. Jake and Alicia did not know what to do. Alicia was afraid. All she could hear was the waterfall. Jake shouted at her to paddle again, but she didn't move. Suddenly, Jake saw a tree branch hanging over the river. He made a lasso from the rope in the boat and threw it over the branch. Luckily, it caught. Then he and Alicia climbed quickly from the canoe to the safety of the tree.

THEMES

Authors write for a reason. Many times, that reason is to express an idea or send a message. This message is called the *theme*. A book may have several themes, but a story often has only one. Deciding the theme of a story is sometimes difficult, but you will most likely find the theme if you ask yourself "What is the author's message?" or "What is the main reason the author wrote this story?"

On Your Own

Below are some ideas that could be themes in a story. Work with a partner to choose the theme about which you would like to write. Once you have chosen a theme, you and your partner will write separate stories that illustrate (show) that theme. When you have finished, read your stories to each other. Discuss how each of you chose to develop the theme. How are your stories alike? How are they different?

It is important to learn how to face difficult challenges.
Good friends are always there when you need them.
Discovering who you are and what you want to do takes time.
The death of someone you love is hard to accept, but you must live on.
Whatever your dreams are, believe in them and make them happen.

Coming Full Circle

Have you ever noticed that a movie often begins in the same way that it ends? The next time you watch a movie or video, look for this technique. Many times the film will open and close in the same place, or with the same people, or a character will speak the same words at the end that were spoken in the beginning. This technique is called *coming full circle*. Can you think of any reasons that it is used so often?

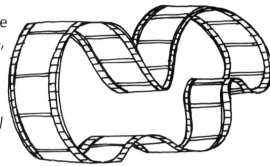

If you read the first few paragraphs and the last few paragraphs of a story or book, you will probably find the very same technique. Coming full circle in writing is just as important as in a movie because it helps the reader feel that the journey has ended—that the story has completed its cycle.

Try this: Choose five books or stories. Read the beginnings and the endings and see how (or if) they come full circle. Remember that this can be done in a number of ways. Before you scan your books, look at the Appendix in the back of this book for some more details on the full circle technique. Choose one of these books and write the words that show the book has come full circle below. Share your findings with a classmate.

Book Title _____

Opening Words _____

_____

_____

Closing Words _____

_____

_____

_____

On Your Own

As you work on a story of your own, think about how you will bring it full circle in the end. To do this, you need to reread your beginning from time to time so that you can design a way for your characters to end up in the same room, say the same words, see the same bus go by, feel the same feelings, etc. To create full circle effects, it helps to visualize your story as a film and then write down what you see, hear, feel, taste, smell, or touch as you begin and end your tale.

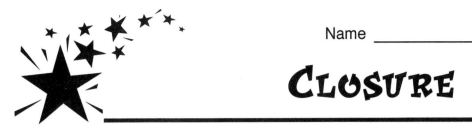

CLOSURE

As you end your story, it is important to provide your readers with *closure*. Closure gives the reader a sense that everything has been completed. It is as though your story is a wonderful gift, and closure is the string that ties the whole package neatly together.

Coming full circle is one technique that helps bring closure to a story. It is also necessary to tell the reader how all the main characters changed as a result of the conflict. In addition, you need to make certain that your readers are not left with any unanswered questions about the plot. The theme of your story should also be clear once you have reached the end. A good way to test your ending is to ask several people of different ages to read your story. If they are uncomfortable with the ending, ask them to tell you why and help you improve your closure technique.

Here is a checklist for closure. Once you have finished a story, ask a classmate to read it and complete the checklist below. If there are any areas which need improvement, work with your reader to rewrite where necessary.

Checklist for Closure

Yes   No

_____ _____ The main character(s) has solved the problem or reached the goal.

_____ _____ I have described what happened to each main character after the problem was solved.

_____ _____ I have returned to the beginning in some way (come full circle).

_____ _____ I have not left any loose ends (unanswered questions) in the plot.

_____ _____ The theme of my story is clear.

Other comments or suggestions:_____

_____

_____

_____

_____

Section 6

Genres

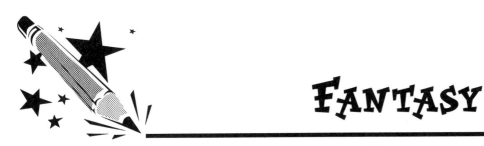

FANTASY

A *fantasy* story is one that could never happen. Such stories contain events, ideas, or even imaginary worlds that do not, and cannot, exist. Often, fantasy stories have magical aspects or include journeys, quests, or dreams. They may have characters such as elves, fairies, leprechauns, demons, wizards, giants, or talking animals (or even talking furniture!) who play an important role in the story. Fantasy stories are fun to write because your imagination can really take off! A good way to begin a fantasy story is to brainstorm "imaginings." Here are some examples:

Imagine what it would be like to . . .

Travel on stardust

be as small as an ant

flow through the human body

discover a magical world beneath the sea

become a wizard

✍ On Your Own

Brainstorm some imaginings of your own. Choose one of them to begin a fantasy story. Create the impossible in your story. Help your main character reach a goal, have an adventure, or learn an important truth. Allow your readers to escape from the limits of everyday life by entering your world of fantasy!

SCIENCE FICTION

You have probably seen many movies and television shows about science fiction topics. *Science fiction* is a type of fictional writing that uses current ideas in science to project what life might be like in the future. The story is still an imaginary tale, but there might be parts of it that could be true 25, 50, or 100 years from now. Often science fiction stories take place in space or on other planets.

Some aspects of life that may be very different in science fiction stories include the following:

Roles of men and women—This means that men and women may have very different types of jobs than they do today, both in the home and outside the home. They might also behave in ways different from ways they behave now.

Family rearing practices—Children may be raised in completely new ways. For example, perhaps they are born in laboratories, or raised together with other children, but not in families.

Transportation methods—The way people get around is always unusual in science fiction stories. Often, space or interplanetary travel takes place using amazing, high-tech machinery. Your imagination can really run wild here!

Type of food—What people eat, and the way they eat it, could be very strange. Maybe they take a certain number of colored crystals every day or get their nourishment from an electrical charge to their bodies.

Homes—These may be underground, floating in space, in the sky—almost anything, anywhere. What is inside homes may also be very unusual, such as beds that float on air, moving sidewalks within the house, or completely computerized houses.

Dress—Futuristic characters really dress funny. They may have to wear oxygen tanks because the atmosphere is so thin. They may be required to wear uniforms or to wear only certain colors. You can dress them any way you like.

On Your Own

Create a character who lives at some date in the future. Give him or her an occupation. Then write a one- to two-page scenario which describes this character as he or she gets up in the morning, works at his/her job, travels to see a friend, etc. As you write, include as many of the categories mentioned above as possible. Remember to gradually paint a picture of this futuristic scene for your reader, instead of just telling him or her what everything is like.

MYSTERIES

"Whodunit" stories are great fun to read. Crafting a mystery story is by no means an easy task, however. To write one well, the author must carefully lay clues for both the "detective" in the story and the reader, without giving away the solution before the very end of the book. Before you attempt to write a mystery story, be certain to read several different types and examine how the authors put together the facts that will solve the mystery. Once you are ready to begin, a guide such as the one below can be used to get you started.

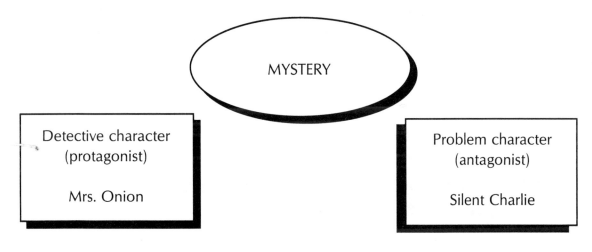

The Mystery of the Stolen Bagels

Protagonist characteristics: Mrs. Onion: *plump, short, owns a bagel bakery, smart, clever, always wears an apron, very observant, wears spectacles with a chain, smells of rose perfume*

Antagonist characteristics: Silent Charlie: *ten-year-old boy, does not talk much, poor, no friends, wears old, dirty clothes, does odd jobs for Mrs. Onion whenever he can to make a little money*

Main mystery: *Suddenly, bagels begin disappearing from the bagel shop. The mystery to be solved: Who is stealing them and why?*

Solution: *Silent Charlie turns out to be the thief, but he is not stealing the bagels for himself. He is taking them to a five-year-old street child, an orphaned girl, whom he has taken under his wing.*

Possible Clues:

1. *Mrs. Onion notices that the bagels always disappear on a day Silent Charlie has done some work for her.*

2. *Silent Charlie begins carrying an old backpack around with him.*

3. One day, Mrs. Onion notices that the backpack looks empty when Silent Charlie comes in, but lumpy when he leaves.

4. Finally, Mrs. Onion follows Silent Charlie. She sees him take the bagels out of his bag and count them, but she does not see him give them to the little girl.

5. The next day, when Silent Charlie comes to work for Mrs. Onion, she questions him about the bagels. Silent Charlie, of course, does not say anything. Mrs. Onion then gets angry and tells him not to come back to her store. Before Silent Charlie leaves that day, however, some more bagels disappear.

Resolution: That evening, when Mrs. Onion is on her way home, she turns a corner and sees Silent Charlie take the bagels out of his bag and give them to the little girl. Suddenly, she understands why he has been stealing from her. She goes over to the two children and asks them both to come and help her at her store. The mystery is solved!

Other notes: The reader will be kept "in the dark" about the reason Silent Charlie is stealing the bagels. This means that the reader will not find out about the little girl until Mrs. Onion finds out, at the very end of the story.

✍ On Your Own

Think of an idea for a mystery story. Remember that there are many types of mysteries: missing people, missing objects, murders, puzzling circumstances (such as *The Riddle of the Cave*), or strange happenings (such as *Mystery at Ghost Cove*). Before you write, plan the basic details of the story as shown in the example above. Have a classmate read your plan and help you critique it before you begin the actual story. As you write, weave important clues into the story so that your readers will stay interested and can feel like detectives along with the character who is solving the mystery.

Animal "Tails"

Many of our favorite books are about animals. Animal stories may be tales of actual animals, stories involving fictitious animals, or wild fantasies in which the animals talk and have journeys of their own. Like all stories, knowing your subject well is important in animal stories. If you wish to write about a dog or a horse and have never observed these animals, it will be difficult to write about them in a realistic way. If that is the case, before you write, you must do observation research. You can do this either by watching actual animals or by viewing movies about the animals. If you feel you know the animal well enough to write about it, you should be able to answer all the questions below:

1. What does the animal look like? Include ears, whiskers, tail, feet, teeth, coloring, fur, eyes, nose, size, weight, special features (mane, claws, etc.), or lack of any of these.

2. Where does the animal usually live? Include what part of the world (or country), what type of "house" it makes or lives in, and what type of climate it likes or needs.

3. What does the animal eat? Include whether it hunts or is hunted, how it catches or gathers its food, how it eats its food, and several types of food it eats.

4. How does the animal move around? Include the method of movement (feet, slides on belly, swims, flies, etc.), adjectives that describe its typical movement (such as swift, careful, proud, unhurried), and how often it moves around (always moving, only when hunting, only in summer, etc.).

5. In what groups does the animal live? Include the social structure of this animal's group, whether or not there is a leader and how it is chosen, and the work that is expected of males, females, or the young.

On Your Own

Once you are certain you know your subject well, decide what type of animal story you would like to tell. Perhaps you know a real-life animal who was a hero or who was rescued from a dangerous situation. Or maybe you would like to create a story about an animal that could be true but is not (fiction). Or you may want to give your animal human qualities, such as the ability to speak or write. Try one of these to create your own animal "tail."

REALISTIC FICTION

Stories that come under the category known as realistic fiction are either stories that could be true, but are not, or stories that contain some facts that are true. A story about a boy who finds a lost puppy, a girl who strives to become an Olympic basketball player, or a family who grows up in a city ghetto are all examples of realistic fiction. When writing these types of stories, it is a good idea to base the story on some experience you, or someone close to you, has had. It is easier to make it seem real to the reader if parts of it actually did occur.

Most realistic fiction has two main purposes: to tell an interesting story and to send an important message. The message that the author is trying to send to the reader is called the *theme*. For example, a story about a boy who finds a lost puppy may have a theme that concerns kindness or friendship. A story about a girl who becomes an Olympic basketball player may have the message that a person should never give up or should follow their dreams. And a story about a family living in a city ghetto may be trying to show that families may be rich in spirit, even though they may not have much money.

When you write realistic fiction, it is a good idea to have in mind what type of theme you would like your story to have. Ask yourself, "What do I want my readers to learn from my story?" This will help you stay focused on your goal as you write.

✍ On Your Own

Start by brainstorming some events that have happened to you, your family, or your friends that might make a good story. Here are some categories to consider:

ACHIEVEMENTS ADVENTURES

DISAPPOINTMENTS

ACTS OF KINDNESS
(given or received)

REALIZATIONS (such as gaining a
new understanding of someone)

Once you have an idea in mind, consider what message (theme) you want to relate through your story. Then you can use the Story Planning Chart in the Appendix to help you organize your ideas more completely. Remember that the characters and dialogue in realistic fiction must be as "real" as the events you create. Ask a classmate to review your work from time to time to make certain the story is progressing in a clear and appropriate way.

HISTORICAL FICTION

The main purpose of historical fiction stories is to give the reader information about a certain time period, person, or event in history. The historical part means that you must include some historical facts in the story. The fiction part means that you can make up some aspects of the story. You can use people who actually lived and have them do things they did not really do or go places that they did not really go; you can make up people and have them do things and go places that actually existed; or you can make yourself a time traveler and take part in history in any way you like!

Like many other types of stories, historical fiction requires some research. Once you decide on a topic, you will need to find out more about the people, the time period, and the events that are connected to that topic. Here are some of the aspects of history that you might include when you write your story:

CLOTHING   WAYS OF SPEAKING

WAYS OF COMMUNICATING

TYPE OF FOOD   TYPE OF GOVERNMENT

TYPE OF HOUSES

IMPORTANT EVENTS OF THAT ERA

FAMOUS PEOPLE OF THAT ERA

METHODS OF TRANSPORTATION

On Your Own

Choose a person, a place, an event, or a time period of history that you would like to explore. Gather some information about your topic from books, films, magazines, or interviews. Make lists of the information you discover in each of the categories mentioned above. Then use the Story Planning Guide in the Appendix of this book to help you map out your historical fiction story.

SPORTS STORIES

Most of us have certain sports that we enjoy more than others. Many of us play on teams or compete, and some of us hope to become successful, or even famous, athletes one day. Stories about real-life or fictitious sports figures often help us continue to strive for our goals, even if our goals do not include a career in sports. This is because people who participate in sports demonstrate discipline, dedication, and desire. They know how to set goals and create programs to reach them. Reading about their lives helps others to do the same.

DO YOU . . .

PLAY BASKETBALL, FOOTBALL, BASEBALL, VOLLEYBALL, TENNIS, LACROSSE, HOCKEY, OR SOCCER?

RIDE HORSES? ICE SKATE? SKI?

RUN TRACK? DO GYMNASTICS?

DO YOU . . .

COMPETE ON A LOCAL, STATE, OR NATIONAL LEVEL?

DO YOU . . .

KNOW SOMEONE WHO HAS ACHIEVED A HIGH LEVEL IN SPORTS?

HAVE A HERO OR HEROINE IN SOME SPORT?

HAVE A DESIRE TO BE AN OLYMPIC OR ALL-STAR ATHLETE?

HAVE A FUNNY, SAD, OR ENCOURAGING STORY TO TELL ABOUT YOUR EXPERIENCE IN A PARTICULAR SPORT?

On Your Own

Write a sports story of your own. Choose a sport in which you have an interest or talent. Remember that when you are writing fiction, you can use events that have actually happened and add whatever else you like. You can also create a story that is completely fictitious. Use the questions above to help you get started. Then use the Story Planning Guide in the Appendix of this book to help you complete your planning.

ADVENTURE!

You have probably already had many adventures in your life. These experiences can make wonderful starting points for fictional adventure stories. You may also have dreamed of taking some adventure—perhaps a voyage into space or to Africa or into the sea. A good adventure story often includes a quest for something, a mystery that must be solved, or interesting exploits by the main character. Stories such as *Huckleberry Finn*, *Indiana Jones*, and *Homeward Bound* are all adventure stories, even though their actual plots are very different.

To begin an adventure story, start by brainstorming ideas in the following areas:

ADVENTURES I HAVE HAD

ADVENTURES PEOPLE I KNOW HAVE HAD

ADVENTURES I WOULD LIKE TO HAVE

Once you have some ideas, choose the one that is most exciting to you to use for your adventure story. Create a main character who will experience the adventure(s) you are planning. Spend some time thinking about the aspects of this character. Because the main character will be the vehicle that takes your readers on the adventure, he, she, or it needs to be a character that will appeal to your audience. Use the character guide below to begin to sketch this character. Then use the Story Planning Guide in the Appendix of this book to help you complete your planning.

Audience: Children (ages _____)?   Teenagers (ages _____)?
          Adults?   Everyone?

Main Character(s): Person? Animal? Other? One or more than one?

Physical Characteristics: (if an animal, describe animal characteristics, such as type of fur, ears, claws, way of moving, etc.)

age   hair color, length, type
weight   height
type of clothing   manner of walking and/or talking
skin color   special features (high cheekbones, freckles, tiny
                                 nose, big ears, brilliant blue eyes, etc.)

Personality Characteristics: These include adjectives that describe your character as well as things he or she does that reveal something about character. For example, is your character shy, bold, talkative, curious, reckless, kind, or smart? Does your character like to read books, get in trouble, follow interesting people, chew gum, say a certain phrase over and over again, write poetry, play a musical instrument, or have a pet?

Other Details: These include anything that might give your readers a better picture of your character such as his or her family information (brothers, sisters, parents, orphan, etc.), where he or she lives (country, city, state, type of house, etc.), or historical information about the character (previous adventures, earlier events in his or her life, etc.).

FRIENDSHIP STORIES

Many of the best stories we read have a theme that concerns friendship. In these stories, friends may go through hard times, discover new things together, grow up sharing experiences, or have exciting adventures. You probably have some good friends with whom you have had special or important experiences. These friends may be your age, or they may be older or younger. To begin your friendship story, use the brainstorming diagram below. To help you get started, an example appears below.

Friend: Lisa
Experience: She stayed with me when I was very sick.
Things I learned or realized: True friends help out even when they may have to give up something or change their own plans. We need friends to help us get through the difficult times in life.

On Your Own

Think of a good friend that has been or is currently important in your life. Then fill in the diagram below. When you begin your story, provide the reader with some background information about your friendship. This information should include how you met, some of the things you have done together, and why you are friends. Slowly lead up to the experience you want the story to be about. By the end of your story, your readers should understand why this person is important to you and what you have learned or realized because of the experience(s) you shared.

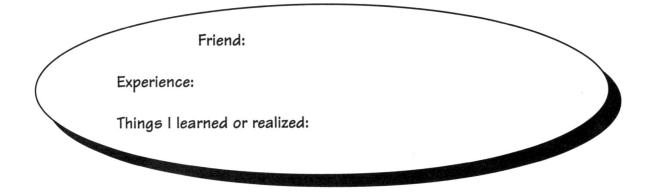

Friend:

Experience:

Things I learned or realized:

FABLES

Fables are short tales that teach some kind of lesson. This lesson is called a *moral*. The moral is written at the end of the fable to make certain the reader understands the lesson that is being taught. The characters in fables are often animals who may do human things like talking. We have taken some of our sayings such as "crying wolf" from fables. Fables are fun to read and fun to write. Here is an example of a fable written by a fifth grader:

The Hero
by Ilana Licht

The gorilla was walking up and down the rough streets, stepping on spiders that were trying to make webs in which to catch their food. On the street where the large gorilla was walking, there was a dark hole. He put one leg in it and fell. A little spider was watching from a distance, where the gorilla couldn't see it.

The friendly spider scurried like a mouse over to the hole. Then it looked around and saw a pitchfork in the hay across the road at the Smith's farm. The spider called one hundred other spiders and asked for their help. They all hurried over to the fork and, working together, lifted it. They walked very slowly back to the hole where the gorilla had fallen. Then they stuck the fork into the hole, and the gorilla held onto the pitchfork.

The spiders pulled and tugged until they got the gorilla out of the hole. The gorilla jumped up and yelled, "I will never step on an insect or animal again!"

And all the spiders cheered!

Moral: Just because you're little doesn't mean you can't do anything.

✍ On Your Own

Write your own fable. Start by thinking of the lesson you want to teach. Next, decide what animals you want to use as characters. Finally, create the situation that must occur for the moral to be taught. Remember to write your moral at the bottom of your fable. Take time to make a nice, color illustration to go with your writing. Share your fable with your classmates.

MYTHS

Make-believe stories that explain how things came to be are called *myths*. They usually tell about the creation of gods or the elements of nature. Most cultures, past and present, have myths that are passed down to their children to help explain the world. Ancient Greek and Roman myths are interesting stories that we often read in school. Native Americans also have many myths that we sometimes study, as do other groups around the world.

An example of a myth written by a fifth-grade student appears on the next page. Read it before you try writing your own myth.

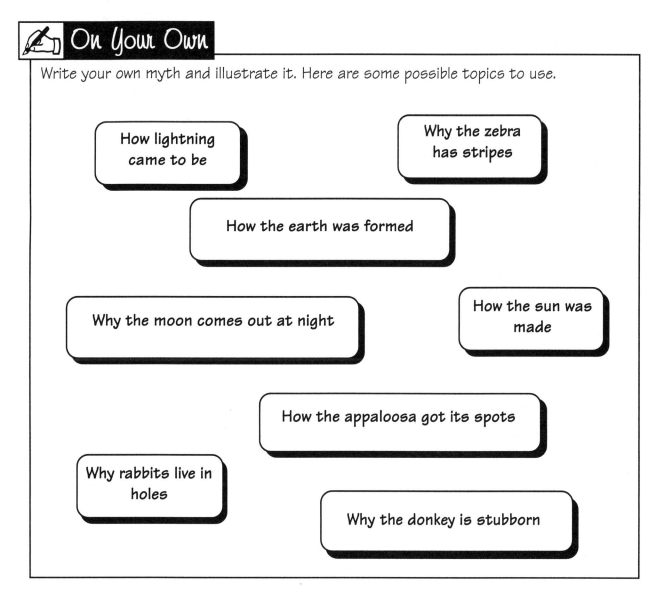

On Your Own

Write your own myth and illustrate it. Here are some possible topics to use.

> How lightning came to be

> Why the zebra has stripes

> How the earth was formed

> Why the moon comes out at night

> How the sun was made

> How the appaloosa got its spots

> Why rabbits live in holes

> Why the donkey is stubborn

Why the Frog Croaks

by Nathaniel Friedman

A very long time ago, before man came to be, the frog was able to speak. But there was one problem. Frog talked too much. He was always distracting other animals from what they were doing.

One day, Lion was busy hunting. Frog didn't care. He went right up to Lion, and scaring all the other animals away, said, "Hello, how are you doing? What did you do yesterday? What are you doing today? What do you plan to do tomorrow? How do you find food, and when do you do it?"

Lion roared back, "I find food by hunting and I was doing it right now! But you talked so loud that you scared all the other animals that I was hunting away! Now, go home and don't bother me again!" Frog walked home slowly, feeling very sad.

The next day, Frog saw Mr. Ant carrying a big bundle of food. Frog walked right up to him and said, "Hello, Mr. Ant. I see you are carrying a big bundle of food! How can you manage such a heavy load? May I have some of the food in your bundle?"

Mr. Ant replied very angrily, "I am working very hard and would appreciate it if you would go home and not bother me again!"

Frog did the same thing to all the other animals and, after a while, they all became very upset. They decided to organize a meeting. They asked the goddess of speech to come to the meeting.

That night, all the animals, including Frog, gathered in a circle around the speech goddess. She said to Frog, "Mr. Frog, I understand you have been disturbing all the other animals by talking too much."

"I have?" asked Frog, amazed. "I hardly ever talk!"

"Well, I am going to have to take away your speech," said the goddess.

Monkey, a close friend of Frog's said, "Take pity on him, Goddess. At least give him some kind of sound!"

"Fine," replied the speech goddess, "instead of speech, I'll give Frog just a simple croak."

Frog tried to debate the issue, but all he could say was, "Croak."

After that, the forest was very peaceful. Nobody disturbed anybody, and actually, it was all very pleasant.

So, sometimes at night, if you hear little croaking sounds among the chirping of the crickets, you'll know that it's our friend Frog, and you'll remember how he got that way!

Name _____

LEGENDS

A story (usually of a person who did something incredible), which has been handed down through history, is known as a legend. As the story is retold, its events become exaggerated. A legend may have a factual basis, but many of its parts are not true. The legend of Johnny Appleseed, who walked all over North America planting apple trees, is a good example. The legend of Paul Bunyan, who is said to have been able to move railroad tracks with his bare hands, is another example. A character in a legend usually has some kind of superhuman powers which are not magical, but beyond the ability of a normal person.

A *legend* is a tale of history and involves amazing abilities or events.

Before you try writing a legend, read some of them. Every culture has its own legends and you may find it interesting to read several legends from different countries. Legends are also called "tall tales" or "folk tales," so be certain to check for them under these categories as well. To help you focus on the ingredients found in legends, fill in the chart below after you have read some legends.

Person	Remembered For	Special Abilities

On Your Own

To begin your legend, think of someone you know, or create a character who is strong, brave, and smart. Exaggerate this person's abilities or give him/her some special, "bigger than life" powers. Then create a situation (problem) that this person must overcome by using his/her "superhuman" abilities.

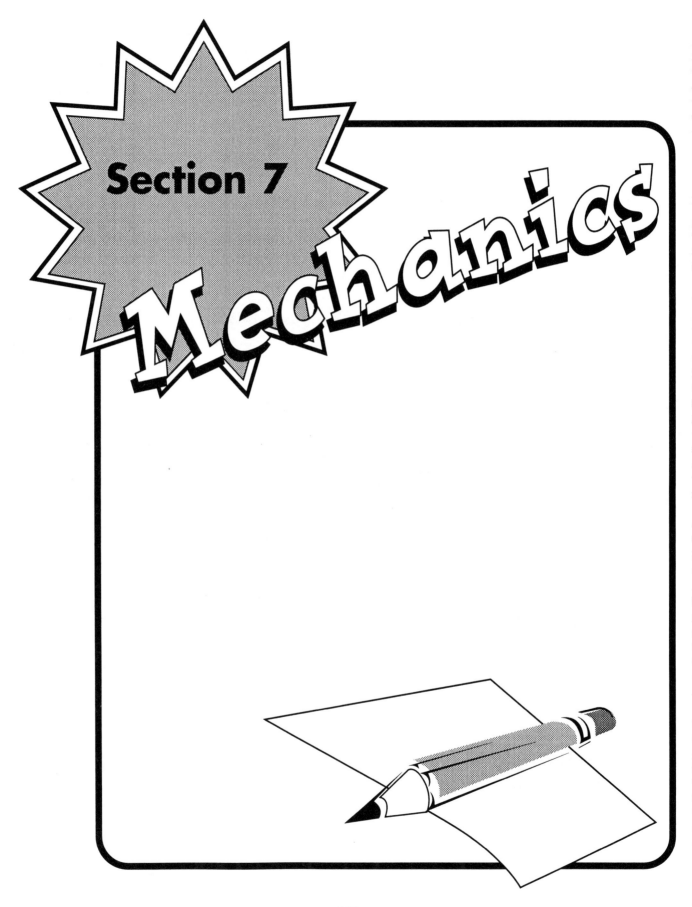

Section 7

Mechanics

FIRST DRAFTS, SECOND DRAFTS, THIRD DRAFTS . . .

A *draft* is a working document. This means that the story or book is *in process*, or not yet completed. Writers often go through many drafts before they are happy with the final product. This can be frustrating, but it is important to understand that almost no piece of writing is finished the first time it is written. There are always parts that need to be improved, expanded, or removed to make the writing flow more smoothly and be more effective.

When you write your first draft, it is wise not to be too picky about actual words or sentences right away. Your ideas are the most important part as you begin to write. When you reread your work, you can make more careful revisions. Write on every other line or double space your draft so that changes can be written where necessary.

Tips

- Always read through your work once you have finished it. Reading it aloud is a particularly good way to spot errors or parts that do not make good sense.
- Ask at least one adult and one person your age to read your work and make suggestions.
- Accept constructive criticism about your work. Other people's ideas provide the perspective of the reader, which is difficult for you to have because you are the writer.
- If possible, put your story away for a few days and then read it again. At that time, you will have a fresh view and be able to make changes more easily.

On Your Own

Choose from the topics below and write a one-page draft. When you are finished, reread your work, making any changes you feel are needed. Then exchange papers with a classmate and critique each other's drafts. The "Second Opinions Checklist" on the next page will help you with your critique. After this, consider the feedback you received and write a second draft.

- How I Saved the Day
- My Pet _____
- The Hero

SECOND OPINIONS

When you read someone else's work, it is important to critique it in a helpful and positive way. Here is a checklist to help you focus on the important questions to ask yourself as you are reading. Be certain to offer suggestions for improvement as you make your critique. If you answer "no" to any of the items below, your explanations should be written in the margin of the draft.

Yes	No	
_____	_____	I can follow the plot of the story well. If "no," explain where and why you are confused.
_____	_____	I can follow the time sequencing and time changes in the story. If "no," explain where and why you cannot follow these transitions.
_____	_____	I have a good picture of the main characters' physical descriptions and their personalities. If "no," explain what is missing.
_____	_____	I understand the message or theme of the story, or the reason the author wrote it. If "no," discuss this problem with the author when you return the draft.
_____	_____	The story comes "full circle" in some way or has good closure at the end. If "no," suggest some ways the author might bring the story "full circle."
_____	_____	The story is well developed. It has enough going on to keep the reader interested. If "no," suggest some improvements.
_____	_____	The sentences in the story are well constructed and easy to follow. If "no," note on the draft any sentence fragments or awkward or confusing sentences.

After you read through the draft and make corrections and suggestions, write a summary comment which uses this model:

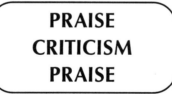

**PRAISE
CRITICISM
PRAISE**

Here is a sample comment which follows the model above:

Jamie, I liked the way you described the setting and the characters. I really felt I had a good picture in my mind of what everything and everyone looked like. (Praise)
It was difficult for me to follow the plot after the diamond was stolen, however. Things seemed to happen too fast and there was not enough explanation. (Criticism)
Overall, though, you have a great beginning and good ideas in this story. (Praise)
Thanks for sharing it with me.
    Diane

EDITING YOUR WORK

It is always a good idea to put your writing away for several days before you try to edit it. The lapse in time helps you to see the piece with a fresh look so you can edit more effectively. The checklist below will assist you as you examine your work. If you answer "no" to any of the items below, go back to your draft and rewrite as necessary.

Yes   **No**

_____ _____ My sentences are clear, well constructed, and make good sense.

_____ _____ My word choices give details which help to create vivid pictures, sounds, smells, flavors, or feelings.

_____ _____ I have not used words or phrases repetitively.

_____ _____ My descriptions of the setting and the characters are complete and give the reader enough information.

_____ _____ My dialogue is realistic, appropriate, and interesting. It adds to the story, rather than filling up space in the story.

_____ _____ There is just enough action in the story to keep it moving along well.

_____ _____ I have followed the idea of a plot line including rising action, a climax, and falling action.

_____ _____ The climax is exciting and clear to the reader.

_____ _____ Paragraphs flow from one to the other. Transitions in time or action are smooth and do not leave the reader with unanswered questions.

_____ _____ The story as a whole makes sense. There are no gaps that the reader must try to fill on his/her own.

_____ _____ The conflict (problem) and the resolution to the conflict (solution) are evident to the reader.

_____ _____ I have used "full circle" elements to open and close my story.

_____ _____ I have tied up all the loose ends to the story. The reader is not left with questions about the plot or what happened to the characters.

_____ _____ My message or theme is clearly presented in the story.

_____ _____ I have proofread my work for errors in punctuation, grammar, and spelling.

PROOFREADING YOUR WORK

After you have edited your draft and rewritten your story at least once, it is time to begin the task of final proofreading. Proofreading involves checking for errors in the following areas:

- spelling
- typing
- punctuation

- sentence construction
- grammatical construction
- dialogue construction

Practice your proofreading skills on the paragraph below. Remember to look for proper use of capitals, commas, periods, apostrophes, question marks, exclamation points, and quotation marks. Check for incomplete sentences (sentence fragments) and run-on sentences. Be certain that all words are spelled correctly, that no typing errors exist, and that correct grammar has been used. Finally, make certain that paragraphs begin in the correct places. If they do not, use the paragraph symbol to show that a new paragraph should begin. You can make all the corrections right on this paper.

It was a lovle day on the beach. AFter we awoke, we quickly threw on our bathing suits and rushed outside into the bright sunshine and grabbed our surfboards and ran into the water To our surprise it was really cold? We stayed in anyway and eventually got used to the temperture. As a big wave came in. My friends surfboard twisted out of his hand and raced to the shore without him. "Too bad, I laughed, as I prepared to catch the next wave in. "Ha, ha, ha," he replied, like it never happens to you. That night we made a bonfire and cooked hot dogs over the open flame. Then we made s'mores with marshmelons, grandma crackers, and chalklate. What a gerat day I cant wait until tomorrow.

DIALOGUE MECHANICS

When you write speaking parts (dialogue) in your stories, there are several punctuation rules you need to remember. These are

1. Start a new paragraph each time a new person speaks.

2. Put quotation marks (" ") around the parts that are spoken.

3. Commas, not periods, follow most speaking parts.

4. In dialogue, periods, commas, exclamation points, and question marks go *inside* the quotation marks.

5. There is no space between the quotation mark at the beginning of the sentence and the first letter. There is no space between the comma (or other ending punctuation) and the quotation mark.

6. There *is* a space after the closing quotation mark and the word which follows it.

Examples:
"Hi Andy," yelled Angela as she raced to catch up with her friend.
"Hey Angie, how's it going?" replied Andy. "Can I carry something for you?"
"That would be great. Thanks!" Angela sighed, and she dumped some of her books into Andy's outstretched arms.

Practice using quotation marks correctly by rewriting the paragraph below on a separate sheet of paper. Use the rules above to help you. (Note: all the punctuation given to you is correct.)

Where are you going Sam asked Cindy. I'm going to Six Flags amusement Park replied Sam. I've never been there and I'm really excited about going. It's a great place Cindy said enthusiastically. My favorite ride is Colossas. What's that Sam asked. It's a gigantic roller coaster. It goes really fast. I rode it seven times when I went last summer Cindy explained. Cool exclaimed Sam. I can't wait to try it! I hope you have a great time, Sam Cindy said warmly. I'll see you tomorrow. Thanks, Cindy, I'm sure I will said Sam.

Appendix

SAMPLES OF INTRODUCTIONS AND CONCLUSIONS
(For use with pages 72-73)

Style 1: Story-like introduction—a dramatic scene

She padded silently across the mesa, the still warm rabbit hanging limp and lifeless from her mouth. The soft morning breeze ruffled her red-gray fur slightly as the sun slowly crawled toward its place in the newborn desert sky. The tips of her small, rounded ears flicked back and forth constantly, listening ahead, behind, and side to side, always alert, ever aware. As she approached her den, the man crouched lower, aiming, ready to shoot when that perfect moment finally came. The she-wolf was now within a few feet of the cave and the man steadied himself, held his breath, and shot. The animal stopped dead at the noise, waited, and hearing nothing else, moved cautiously inside the den to her expectant cubs. The man smiled. He'd finally managed the perfect picture of the Mexican wolf returning from the hunt—a shot he'd been planning for several weeks.

The man described above was lucky. He had the opportunity to view the Mexican wolf in its own wild habitat. Few will have this chance, perhaps none at all, for the Mexican wolf is no longer a common site in nature. Loss of habitat due to human expansion is one reason for the decline of these stately animals. Their populations have also dwindled because they have been mercilessly hunted. All too often it has been the man with the gun, instead of the man with the camera, who has shot the wolf. For the Mexican wolf, these factors have been disastrous, and there are now fewer than 50 of these noble creatures left in the wild. Without careful plans to preserve the Mexican wolf, it will soon become extinct and no man, hunter, or photographer will glimpse the red-gray forms streaking across the mountain top nor hear the haunting howls set against the background of a full, white moon.

Style 1: Story-like conclusion—a dramatic scene

To be able to see the Mexican wolf padding across the desert as it has for centuries, it is imperative that steps be taken to preserve this species. Wolves now depend on humans to protect their habitat so that they can continue to exist. Without this protection, the beautiful Mexican wolf will no longer raise its cubs in sheltered mountain caves nor skillfully hunt an injured deer. It will no longer rest in the shade of a mesquite tree nor roam the desert terrain in search of water. And it will no longer lift its majestic voice to the waning moon. Indeed, we will be left only with the haunting memory of its cry, a brilliant reminder of our failure to save it.

Style 2: Background information about the species in general

The wolf is an animal about which many myths, stories, and fairy tales have been told. Sadly, the wolf has often been portrayed as "the big, bad wolf," an idea which carries little truth. In fact, even though there has never been a documented attack on humans by wolves in North America, the belief that these animals are dangerous to people continues. In truth, the wolf is content to live away from humans and rarely visits human-inhabited areas. Contrary to many stories, wolves hunt only when in need of food and usually kill the young, old, or injured animals, helping nature to keep a good balance between species' populations. Often, because they have been so misunderstood, wolves have been hunted. Due to this overhunting and to habitat destruction as well, some types of wolves have become endangered. The beautiful red-gray Mexican wolf is one such animal. Unless something is done to help this species immediately, it may be lost from the face of the earth forever, for there are fewer than 50 left in the wild.

Style 2: Returning to background information about the species in general

It is clear that something must be done to save the Mexican wolf before it vanishes forever. Wolves, including the Mexican wolf, have been hunted for their pelts and because people have believed they were dangerous. They have lost much of their needed space as humans have expanded their own living areas. Wolves need large areas of protected land in which to roam and hunt. Unless we pay attention to their needs, we may soon place many species of wolves on the endangered list. In addition, there is still a need for education about the true habits and behaviors of wolves. Without such awareness and action, the "big, bad wolf" will be neither big, nor bad, he will simply be gone.

Style 3: Background information about the larger topic

The world is an amazing place, full of a wonderful variety of plants and animals. On every continent one can see an array of life particular to that certain place. This diversity of life brings not only beauty to our existence, but provides a large gene pool from which new life springs. As the human population expands, however, this diversity among living things becomes more fragile. The loss of habitats for many animals due to the building of new homes and businesses has caused animal populations to decline, in some cases, to dangerously low levels. Some species have even become extinct and others are in immediate danger of becoming so. The Mexican wolf is one such species. There are fewer than 50 of these noble creatures left in the wild, and it has become essential to act on their behalf before they are lost forever.

Style 3: Returning to background information about the larger topic

In conclusion, it has become extremely important to save the Mexican wolf before it becomes extinct. With only 50 animals left in the wild, conservation of this species must begin now. There is a need for preservation of the few remaining habitats. Breeding programs in zoos and preserves must be practiced to increase the species numbers. Laws must be enacted to protect the wolf and punish the hunter. Education programs must be developed to help people understand the wolf and the need to preserve it. Without such measures, we will not only lose the Mexican wolf, we will lose yet another piece of our wonderfully diverse world—a world which cannot continue to exist if its variety of life is threatened. Man cannot live by man alone; we are intricately connected to all life, and we must be dedicated to preserving all that we have.

Book Report Guidelines

(For use with page 75)

Begin by describing the **setting.**

Next, introduce the main **characters** in a brief (one typed page) **plot summary.** Make certain you give an idea of the physical description of the characters, as well as their personalities.

Then analyze the characters. What were their functions, their purposes?

Go on to the **conflict(s)** and **resolutions(s).** Include the **climax,** discussing when and how it occurs.

Now discuss the **theme(s)** of the book. Does the title of the book tie in with any of the themes? If so, how? **Use quotations** from the book **to support your ideas** about the themes.

Try to discover the **significance (importance) of the title** of the book and explain it in your report. When reading, mark the pages where the title is mentioned. Why did the author choose this title? Use quotations again if they support your ideas.

Finally, explain how the book comes **full circle.** Read the first few pages of the first chapter and the first few pages of the last chapter. Look for similarities in the setting, the character's actions, or the character's attitudes between the beginning and the ending of the book. For example, if a story opens on the third floor of a hospital, does it close there as well? If the character had a journey to make, is he or she back to the starting point in some way by the end of the story?

A story may come full circle by ending **not exactly** the same way it began, but in a similar way. For example, if a story about a woman opened with her being born, the book would come full circle if it closed with that woman having a child of her own.

Coming full circle is like tying the ends of a ribbon around a package. The book is the package, and the full circle elements are the ribbon. A story must have **closure** for the reader to feel things have ended properly. Coming full circle often provides a book with the closure it needs. When you find examples of how the book comes full circle, quote the passages that show this in your book report.

Crafting a Story

(For use with the Genres section)

THE BEGINNING:
—Catches the interest of the reader
—Introduces characters; hero/heroine (protagonist is usually the first one introduced)
—Sets the stage—time, place, social setting
—Sets the mood—funny, sad, scary, thrilling
—Introduces the problem
—Foreshadows possible complications and solutions

THE MIDDLE:
—Protagonist takes action to solve problem, is blocked several times, but continues to try to find answers or reach the goal.
—Techniques which can be used to keep the story moving:
    —suspense
    —characterization
    —dialogue
    —rhyme
    —repetition
    —contrast
    —accumulation of events, problems, data

THE ENDING:
—The ending must be believable. It is likely to have happened given the particular characters and their circumstances.
—The protagonist should have accomplished the goal or solved the problem on his or her own.
—The reader should be left with a sense of completeness or closure.
—Books for younger children should have a reassuring ending, while books for ages 12 and up can be more open ended, with maybe a question or two not answered. Cynicism and depressing or hopeless endings should be reserved for young adult books (ages 14 and up).
—The story should come full circle. The climax comes at a point nearer to the end of the story, but there follows a resolution which ties up most loose ends.

Plotting a Story

Five Steps to Follow
(For use with the Genres section)

STEP 1: ESTABLISH SETTING, CHARACTERS, AND POINT OF VIEW

Setting
—When (in what time period) will the story take place?
—What time of year?
—How many hours, days, months, years will the story cover?
—Where will the story take place? What city/country/room? Inside someone's head? In a fantasy world? In outer space?
—How many different settings do you anticipate throughout the course of the story?
—How will you paint your setting? Use literary techniques which aid the reader in "seeing" the setting and "feeling" the setting.

Characters
—Who will the main character(s) be? Who will be the protagonist (the leading character or hero/heroine)? Who will be the antagonist (the person or element opposed, or against, the protagonist)?
—Character type: animal/human/boy/girl/man/woman/other? Why do you choose the ones you do? Make certain you have a reason for your choices.
—How many characters? Be careful not to have too many because the reader may have trouble keeping them straight. The older the children reading the book, the more characters they can handle in a story.
—What will their names be? Do not use names which start with the same letter for main characters as it gets confusing. Use appropriate names—for example, a story about a Mexican boy would not feature a child named Pierre.
—How old are the characters? This depends a bit on your audience. In general, children tend to read books about characters who are slightly older than they are. Adults, of course, read all types of books, regardless of the characters' ages.
—Are they good characters or bad characters? No one is ever all good or all bad (except, perhaps, in fairy tales). To be believable, a good character must have a little bad in him/her, and a bad character must have a little good in him/her. The actions of these characters should be appropriate to the character; they cannot do/think things they would be totally unlikely to do/think, or the character will have little credibility.
—Are the characters too stereotyped? Do all the females work inside the home and cater to men? Do all the men have macho attitudes? Do all the black or minority characters have positions inferior to whites? Balance your characters so that they are believable, but not overly predictable in this way.

Point of View

—First person: Use of *I*. The story is told from one character's viewpoint only, as though the author were that particular character.

—Second person: Use of *You*. Second person point of view is rarely used and difficult to use effectively. The character may be addressing the reader. It is found in *Choose Your Own Adventure* stories.

—Third person limited: Use of *he* and *she*. The story is told from one character's viewpoint only, as though the author were observing that particular character.

—Omniscient: All knowing. All characters' points of view are told. The reader knows the inside of everyone's mind. This point of view is very difficult to do effectively.

STEP 2: DEFINE THE PROBLEM OR GOAL AND DETERMINE THEMES

—What does the main character want and why?

—The problem or goal must be a meaningful one, one that is worth writing a story around.

—What messages or main ideas (themes) do you want to give your reader? Do you want to teach something? Make a comment on something? State a philosophy? How will your characters accomplish these aims? Which character(s) will be your main vehicle(s) for transmission of these messages?

STEP 3: CREATE CONFLICT

Types of Conflict

—Human vs. Human: the main character is opposed in some way to another character or characters. (External)

—Human vs. Nature: the main character is opposed by some force of nature, such as a blizzard or a drought or a brush fire. (External)

—Human vs. Self: the main character is opposed to himself/herself and fights some type of inner battle. (Internal)

Points to Remember

—The story may have several types of conflict within it. For example, there may be both Human vs. Human (external) and Human vs. Self (internal) or any of the other combinations.

—What will prevent the main character from solving his/her problem or achieving the goal? Something must stand in the way so that the protagonist can rise above it and emerge victorious.

—What does the protagonist do about the obstacles he or she faces?

—Are there complications which arise as a result of the protagonist trying to surmount the obstacles? If so, what are they and what is to be done about them?

—To what crisis do these struggles lead?

STEP 4: RESOLVE THE CONFLICT

—What is the climax (the most exciting part of the story)? How does the protagonist arrive at the climax?

—Does the protagonist accomplish his/her goal or solve the problem? If so, how? If not, why not?

STEP 5: COME FULL CIRCLE

—To provide closure for the story, the story must wind its way back to the original setting. This may be achieved by physically returning to the opening setting or by having the protagonist arrive at some conclusion or realization which refers in some way to his/her starting point.

Story Planning Sheet

Major Setting(s):

Main Characters:

Protagonist:

Antagonist:

Others:

Problem or Goal:

Point of View: (first person, second person, third person, omniscient)

Type of conflict(s): (human vs. human, human vs. environment, human vs. self)

Theme(s)

Plot summary including conflict (problem), climax, and resolution (solution):
(20 sentences or less)

Lovely Language Quiz

(For use with the Creative Writer's Toolbox section)

Match the definition on the right to the term on the left.

_____ 1. alliteration

_____ 2. onomatopoeia

_____ 3. hyperbole

_____ 4. metaphor

_____ 5. simile

_____ 6. symbol

_____ 7. personification

_____ 8. rhyme

_____ 9. repetition

_____ 10. oxymoron

A. words such as _late_ and _date_

B. a comparison using _like_ or _as_

C. repetition of beginning consonant sounds

D. words such as _buzz_ or _clang_

E. a direct comparison in which something is said to be something else

F. a concrete (often visual) representation of an idea or concept

G. when a nonliving object is said to have the characteristics or actions of a person or living thing

H. an exaggeration for effect

I. two words used together that mean the opposite of each other when used separately

J. the use of a word, phrase, or idea over and over again

Write the letter of the correct lovely language term used in each sentence below.

a—alliteration   b—onomatopoeia   c—hyperbole   d—metaphor

e—simile   f—symbol   g—rhyme   h—repetition

i—personification   j—oxymoron

_____ 1. The night was a terrible monster.

_____ 2. Lovely Lady Linda looks like a lioness.

_____ 3. The loud buzz of the chainsaw was deafening.

_____ 4. The wind grabbed me and threw me against the wall.

_____ 5. The sun sparkled on the sea like a crystal diamond.

_____ 6. The explosion created a bright darkness all around us.

_____ 7. School is fun/but I wish I were done!

_____ 8. I send you this dove, hoping the war is now over.

_____ 9. And so I go/though hard it is/and so I travel on/And so I find my path again/And so on/And so on . . . .

_____ 10. He was so ugly he made Godzilla look beautiful!

Answer these questions on another sheet of paper.

1. How is a symbol different from a simile or a metaphor?

2. Choose a symbol for yourself. Explain why you have chosen this as your symbol.

Mechanics Quiz

(For use following the Mechanics section)

Part I: Expand each sentence according to the directions.

1. Add two adjectives to: The dog barked at the boy.

   _____

2. Add two adverbs to: The dog whined and growled as he ate his food.

   _____

3. Change the noun in this sentence: The dog was mean.

   _____

4. Add a prepositional phrase to: The dog barked.

   _____

5. Change the verb in this sentence: The dog barked.

   _____

6. Write a three-word, noun-verb sentence on the first line below. Then expand it into a more interesting sentence using three of the techniques above.

   _____

   _____

   _____

Part II: On a separate sheet of paper, rewrite the following conversation using the correct rules for conversations. Be certain to put in any necessary punctuation. (All the punctuation that is given to you is already correct.) Replace three of the five "saids" with more interesting words.

Hello, Mugwump Swampman said happily. I've been waiting for you. You have? What for? said Mugwump as he jumped over the slippery rocks to Swampman's mud puddle. Because, I just got my new issue of *Swampmuck* magazine and I am on the cover! Don't I look positively disgusting, Mugwump?! Swampman said excitedly as he thrust the magazine into Mugwump's face. Indeed, you do, Swampman, said Mugwump. Wherever did you get that horrible piece of rotted seaweed to drape around your head? Oh, there's lots of that junk around here Swampman said You can always find something utterly repulsive in a swamp, you know. I mean, why else would they call it *Swampmuck* magazine?

Form Poetry Quiz

(For use with the Poetry section)

Directions: Place the letter of the type of poetry in the blanks which describe it below. You may use more than one letter for some definitions.

A. haiku   B. diamante   C. concrete   D. cinquain   E. tanka   F. limerick

_____ 1. Has a definite rhyme scheme

_____ 2. Has five lines

_____ 3. Is an extension of the haiku

_____ 4. Is shaped like a diamond

_____ 5. Has to do with opposites

_____ 6. Has to do with synonyms

_____ 7. Has to do with a single thought, usually about nature

_____ 8. Is usually funny

_____ 9. Is shaped like its subject

_____ 10. Follows a strict syllable pattern

11. Write a four-line poem with the rhyme scheme of abab.

   _____

   _____

   _____

   _____

12. Write a two-line poem showing end rhyme.

   _____

   _____

13. Write a two-line poem showing internal rhyme.

   _____

   _____

14. Write a diamante OR a cinquain on the back of this page.

15. Which type or form of poetry is LEAST like the other types? In what ways is it different? (Use the back to continue your answer.)

Answer Key

Rhyme Scheme   **page 14**

fall	a
call	a
mind	b
time	b

Thesauri   **page 26**

1. honest
2. tasty
3. agreeable
4. desirable
5. suitable

Ballads   **page 42**

1. a new love (girlfriend) of the Seaside Sailor
2. The speaker is female. She is a reflective (thinking) person. She loves the sailor. She wants to understand the sailor's past.
3. He has had past loves. He has lost in love. He thinks about the past. He loves the sea. He is courageous. He has a sadness about him.
4. The Seaside Sailor has a new love. She notices that he is melancholy. She wonders about his past loves. She wants him to know she will not leave him and loves him truly.
5. All five answers are "yes."

Proofreading Your Work   **page 106**

It was a lovely day on the beach. After we awoke, we quickly threw on our bathing suits and rushed outside into the bright sunshine. Then we grabbed our surfboards and ran into the water. To our surprise it was really cold! We stayed in anyway and eventually got used to the temperature. As a big wave came in, my friend's surfboard twisted out of his hand and raced to the shore without him.

"Too bad," I laughed, as I prepared to catch the next wave in.

"Ha, ha, ha," he replied, "like it never happens to you."

That night we made a bonfire and cooked hot dogs over the open flame. Then we made s'mores with marshmallows, graham crackers, and chocolate. What a great day! I can't wait until tomorrow!

Dialogue Mechanics   **page 107**

"Where are you going, Sam?" asked Cindy.

"I'm going to Six Flags Amusement Park," replied Sam. "I've never been there and I'm really excited about going."

"It's a great place!" Cindy said enthusiastically. "My favorite ride is Colossas."

"What's that?" Sam asked.

"It's a gigantic roller coaster. It goes really fast. I rode it seven times when I went last summer," Cindy explained.

"Cool!" exclaimed Sam. "I can't wait to try it!"

"I hope you have a great time, Sam," Cindy said warmly. "I'll see you tomorrow."

"Thanks, Cindy, I'm sure I will," said Sam.

Lovely Language Quiz   **page 118**

1. C
2. D
3. H
4. E
5. B
6. F
7. G
8. A
9. J
10. I

1. d
2. a
3. b
4. i
5. a, e
6. j
7. g
8. f
9. h
10. c

1. A simile or metaphor makes a comparison between two things, usually between things that are not necessarily associated with each other. It is used to show how unlike things may actually be alike. A symbol, however, is a concrete object used to represent a more abstract idea. A symbol often comes to be synonymous with the idea it is used to represent.
2. Answers will vary.

Mechanics Quiz   **page 119**

Part II

"Hello, Mugwump," Swampman cried happily. "I've been waiting for you."

"You have? What for?" asked Mugwump as he jumped over the slippery rocks to Swampman's mud puddle.

"Because, I just got my new issue of *Swampmuck* magazine and I am on the cover! Don't I look positively disgusting, Mugwump?!" Swampman said excitedly as he thrust the magazine into Mugwump's face.

"Indeed, you do, Swampman," said Mugwump. Wherever did you get that horrible piece of rotted seaweed to drape around your head?"

"Oh, there's lots of that junk around here," Swampman replied. "You can always find something utterly repulsive in a swamp, you know. I mean, why else would they call it *Swampmuck* magazine?"

Form Poetry Quiz   **page 120**

1. F
2. D, F
3. E
4. B
5. B
6. D
7. A, E
8. F
9. C
10. A, E
11. Answers will vary.
    | I have a pony | a |
    | Who's very small | b |
    | He's a little bony | a |
    | And not too tall | b |
12. Answers will vary.
    I like chocolate and candy
    Sweets are dandy!
13. Answers will vary.
    The bat and the cat
    Stood and sat

14. Answers will vary. See pages on diamante and cinquain for proper formats and content.
15. Concrete poetry is least like the others. It is most different because it has the fewest rules. It does not have to be about a specific thing, it does not have to have a certain number of lines or syllables, and it does not have to contain rhymes.